DARING DAUGHTERS
St. Augustine's Feisty Females
1565–2000

❧

by Karen Harvey

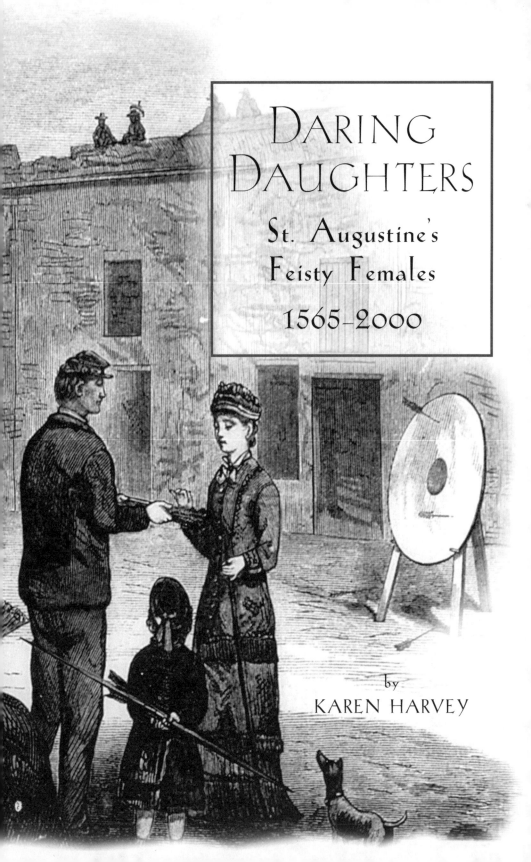

DARING DAUGHTERS

St. Augustine's Feisty Females

1565-2000

by

KAREN HARVEY

For information write: The Donning Company/Publishers, 184 Business Park Drive, Suite 206, Virginia Beach, VA 23462.

Steve Mull, General Manager
B. L. Walton Jr., Project Director
Dawn V. Kofroth, Assistant General Manager
Sally Clarke Davis, Editor
Marshall McClure, Senior Graphic Designer
Scott Rule, Director of Marketing

Library of Congress Cataloging-in-Publication Data

Harvey, Karen G., 1944–
      Daring daughters : St. Augustine's feisty females, 1565–2000 / by Karen Harvey.
         p. cm.
      Includes bibliographical references (p.   ) and index.
      ISBN 1-57864-173-X
         1. Women—Florida—Saint Augustine—Biography. 2. Women—Florida—Saint Augustine—History. 3. Women social reformers—Florida—Saint Augustine—Biography. 4. Women social reformers—Florida—Saint Augustine—History. I. Title.

   HQ1439.S18 H37 2002
   305.4'09759'18—dc21

                                                                      2002025609

**Printed in the
United States of America**

CONTENTS

ACKNOWLEDGMENTS

The names of most of the folks contributing to this book appear in the text of the stories and in the endnotes. Contributors include people such as Latrell Mickler, who formed a fondness for her ancestor Manuela; Dick and Yvonne Punnett who, with Owene Weber, turned their lives upside down searching for lost soul Abbie Brooks; and Kat Twine who first shared her story with me more than a decade ago.

Virginia Hassenflu was the entertaining co-conspirator behind the unfolding saga of the City Gate. George W. Gibbs IV was a wealth of unexplored information about the Kingsley and Gibbs families. To these and all those listed in notes and interviews I give my heartfelt thanks.

The staff and volunteers at the St. Augustine Historical Society Research Library, in particular Charles Tingley, Lesley Wilson, and Bill Temme, were most helpful and generous of their time. Superintendent Gordie Wilson and members of his staff at the Castillo de San Marcos were instrumental in helping me find information and photos. Joanne Moore opened the archives at Flagler College for information related to the "Flagler Women." To all I express my appreciation.

The idea for a book about the women of St. Augustine came from Nadia Ramautaur who contributed to the stories about Dominga de Zèspedes and Catalina Morain. I thank her for sharing her interest in this worthwhile project.

As always. I thank my family members John, Kristina, Jason, and my mother "Eagle-Eye" Elinor Davis for their support and "Eagle-Eye" proofreading expertise.

No one stands beside me as staunchly and loyally as Roberta "Sherlock" Butler whose contributions go above and beyond the call of duty and whose friendship remains strong after many years of collaboration. Thank you, my friend.

INTRODUCTION

They are sweet, smug, tough, genteel, and always daring. The *Daring Daughters* of St. Augustine did not necessarily make a name for themselves as significant historic figures. In fact, most did not aspire to such a distinction. Some courageously faced life's obstacles; others willfully shaped their futures to suit their own desires. Whether their historic contributions were by default or intent, they left their mark.

Antonia, perhaps the first Native American woman to be mentioned in history books written by European males, made a name for herself through her pride and resilience.

Anna Jai Kingsley, the daughter of African royalty, was sold into slavery but surfaced from iniquity to become a prosperous property owner.

Shortly after the Civil War Lucy Abbott made her mark as a neighborhood developer before the word *developer* was coined by man or woman.

A trilogy begins with twice-widowed Clarissa Fairbanks Anderson of Florida's Territorial Period and early statehood days. She, her daughter-in-law, and granddaughter all shaped St. Augustine during a century-and-a-half time period of service.

A summary of the women in millionaire Henry Morrison Flagler's life includes contributions of his mother, sister, and daughter as well as the influence of his three wives. They were all instrumental in guiding the visionary through his lifetime of building a fortune and creating the golden age of St. Augustine, Florida.

People laughed at or with ebullient Diamond Lil when she swept into town in the 1920s creating a furor while launching the Fountain of Youth tourist attraction.

Kat Twine represents more difficult times as she proved she had the right stuff during the turbulent Civil Rights demonstrations of the 1960s.

The modern-day heroines are women who came first: Peggy Ready, the first female county court judge; Ramelle Petroglou, the first female mayor; Peggy Caraway Cottle, the first female deputy sheriff and others. These women represent those who stepped forth in a "good ol' boys" town and took their places in jobs and careers never before entered by members of the female gender.

The tea party of 1900 that saved a historic landmark and the boarding house run by women whose names will be eternally linked with a historic home are just a few of the stories compiled to represent women of the Ancient City. Each tale is unique and each is a lesson for humanity.

The daring daughters are survivors.

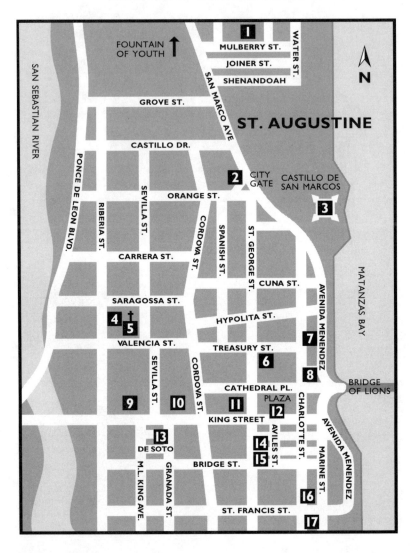

1. North City (Abbott Tract)
2. City Gate
3. Castillo de San Marcos
4. Location of Kirkside
5. Memorial Presbyterian Church
6. Dr. Peck (Peña-Peck) House
7. Monsoon Motel
8. Catalina Morain's place of residence
9. Markland
10 Hotel Ponce de León (Flagler College)
11. Government House
12. Plaza de la Constitución
13. Location of Mather-Perit Church
14. Segui Kirby-Smith House
15. Ximénez-Fatio House
16. González-Alvarez House (Oldest House)
17. St. Francis Barracks

Mary Lily Kenan sits on the lap of her husband, millionaire Henry Morrison Flagler. The newlyweds settled in Palm Beach, Florida, after their 1901 wedding. Photo courtesy of the Flagler College Archives.

CHAPTER I

Fighting the Frontier

❦

ANTONIA
Between Two Cultures (1560s)

The Indian princess sat poised and attentive beside her brother, Chief Carlos of the Calusa Indian tribe. She watched the approach of the Spanish conquistadors led by Don Pedro Menéndez de Avilés, the renowned Captain General of the Seas, now the Adelantado (Governor) of La Florida. Soon he will be my husband, she thought, not daring to move as the soldiers drew near.

The princess was the first woman to emerge with a definitive image and personality after Spanish colonization of La Florida. She was a Native American given a Spanish name and, as Doña Antonia, she would play a significant part in the early days of European settlement in the New World.

Antonia appeared in the chronicles documenting Menéndez' expeditions in the New World. One journal was written by Gonzalo Solís de Merás, Menéndez' brother-in-law who accompanied him on the expedition that resulted in the founding of St. Augustine in September 1565. Bartolomé Barrientos, a contemporary of Menéndez, wrote a second account in 1567. In both, Antonia is portrayed as a complex woman. A first impression revealed a woman discreet and quiet. Later she became spirited, but remained obedient—a woman willing to please, but only on her own terms.

The Indian princess had been chosen by Carlos to be Menéndez' bride. She was prepared to accept him and the challenges ahead of her. She knew some Spanish, learned from sailors shipwrecked in her village in the years before the arrival of Menéndez. She was willing to convert to Catholicism and had eagerly awaited Menéndez' arrival to her village. Menéndez, however, knew nothing of the marriage plan.

It was in late February 1566 when Menéndez' fleet of seven vessels with five hundred men sailed into Charlotte Harbor. The bay provided entry to the Calusa villages just north of current-day Ft. Myers that was, prior to Spanish exploration, known by the Indian name of Escampaha.

The Spanish name *Carlos* had been taken by the current chief's father in honor of then Spanish King Charles V and passed down to his son, the reigning *cacique,* or chief, of the Calusa tribes known by Indians and Europeans alike as King Carlos.

It was Menéndez' mission, as decreed by King Philip II of Spain, to colonize the Spanish-claimed land called Florida. Previous explorers attempted to gain a foothold in the New World, but failed, largely due to hostilities between the European newcomers and the Native Americans. St. Augustine was Menéndez' first settlement and the only one to survive. He was slowly establishing outposts along the East Coast of Florida and now was about to meet with the great Calusa chief in the name of peace and with the hopes of gaining new converts to Catholicism.

His objectives in the Calusa Nation also included rescuing numerous shipwrecked Spaniards who had been held captive by the Indians. After releasing the few prisoners still alive, Carlos invited Menéndez to celebrate with him. Menéndez agreed and took with him an entourage with flags flying, musicians playing fifes, drums, trumpets, harps, and fiddles—and two hundred soldiers.

The ceremony took place in the chief's Great House, a thatch-roofed structure large enough to accommodate two thousand people. Menéndez entered followed by twenty of his men. On a raised dais in the center sat Carlos and a woman whom the Spaniards assumed was the chief's wife. Both were obviously figures of authority and sat with great dignity.

Carlos and the woman greeted Menéndez with palms turned upward, a sign of welcome. Menéndez responded and was rewarded by joyous singing and dancing by the Indians as he sat with Carlos and the princess who was described by chroniclers as about thirty-five years old, not handsome, although quite dignified. When the music stopped, Menéndez pulled out a piece of paper on which he had written a little speech in the Calusa language. Believing the woman to be the chief's principal wife, Menéndez proceeded to compliment her beauty. Quickly an interpreter pulled him aside and corrected his error explaining that the woman was Carlos' sister and was to be given to the Adelantado as *his* wife.

Shocked, Menéndez objected stating he could not marry a

non–Christian. Excusing himself, he spoke quietly with his own men reminding them he had a Spanish wife and could not consent to such "sinning" whether or not Antonia was a Christian.

Carlos, however, made it clear that the Adelantado must take his sister as a wife if there was to be peace between his people and the Spaniards.

The princess watched the activity with concern. "He does not want me," she thought. "I must do something. My brother will be angry if the great leader does not accept me as his wife. He will kill the Adelantado, and I do not want that to happen."

At this point she broke her silence for the first time. Believing the major issue was her lack of religious training, she boldly proclaimed she understood Catholicism and would be willing to convert. She stated that

FERNANDINA
FT. GEORGE ISLAND
MAYPORT
TALLAHASSEE
JACKSONVILLE
ST. AUGUSTINE
ST. JOHNS RIVER
NEW SMYRNA
GULF OF MEXICO
CAPE
TAMPA
CANAVERAL
LAKE
OKEECHOBEE
PORT
CHARLOTTE
FORT MYERS
PALM
BEACH
CALUSA NATION
MIAMI
ATLANTIC
OCEAN

FLORIDA

if Menéndez doubted her sincerity he should take her to Havana for further religious instruction. Menéndez' men were equally insistent that their leader comply with the wishes of the chief as they feared for their lives should Menéndez refuse. Menéndez, realizing he could not afford to offend the chief, agreed. The women traveling with the Spanish expedition came forward and took charge of the princess. After she was bathed and dressed in suitable clothing, she was baptized and given the name Doña Antonia, in honor of St. Anthony, who Menéndez believed guided him to the village where the shipwrecked captives were held. Nowhere in known sources is her Indian name given. She gains her persona only after adopting Christianity as Doña Antonia.

According to an unpublished portion of historian Albert Manucy's book on Menéndez, Antonia "endured the ministrations with her dignity intact." He continued with a description of a feast in the Spanish camp that included much music and dancing. Menéndez sat with Antonia and, conversing in her limited Spanish with the aid of an interpreter, they became acquainted with one another. "He found many things to say which pleased her," Manucy wrote, "and he was himself intrigued by her discreet quietness."

Reports at this point differ dramatically. Solís de Merás writes that Carlos prepared a room for the Adelantado and his sister and she "awaked in the morning joyous and very much pleased." This very obvious referral to consummating the "marriage" is in contradiction to other accounts by Barrientos and Manucy which indicate Menéndez agreed to take Antonia as a wife, but she must first go to Havana and learn the ways of the Catholic religion. He would provide her with a home and teachers who would instruct her in the sacred beliefs. At no time is there mention of a ceremony uniting them in marriage, although the Indians considered them to be husband and wife. It was not unusual for them to view it as such as their culture practiced polygamous unions. The Spaniards simply accepted the situation, treating it with great delicacy.

Antonia remained in Havana as the Adelantado sailed back to St. Augustine and visited the northern settlement at Fort Caroline near the mouth of present St. Johns River. He also traveled north into the Indian territory of Gaul. In May 1566, Menéndez returned to Havana on business and to inquire about Antonia's progress. Shortly after his arrival he attended a party in the home of Antonia's guardians, Don Alonso de Rojas and his wife. Although Antonia was happy to see her "husband" she grew quiet and sad during the evening.

Watching him converse easily with his Spanish compatriots, Antonia felt alone and helpless. "I was given to him as a wife, yet he ignores me. I must tell him how I feel." She knew he was aware of her presence, yet she could not approach the great leader. When she saw he was ready to come to her, she struggled to calm her emotions, desperately wanting to tell him of her despair, but fearing rejection.

Menéndez urged her to disclose her unhappiness, asking if she wasn't content in the home of her host family. She momentarily deferred to him, agreeing she was well treated. Then, as he insisted on knowing the cause of her sadness, her emotions surfaced and she blurted out that "she wished that God might kill her, because when they landed the Adelantado had not sent for her to take her to his house, to eat and sleep with him."[1]

Menéndez, still a religious Catholic married to Ana Maria de Solís in Spain, had agreed to accept Antonia as his "bride" in the name of diplomacy. Now, his situation required defensive tactics.

Using a fictitious excuse that sailors cannot sleep with their wives until eight days had elapsed following their return from sea, he tried to appease Antonia by promising to take her back to Florida on the next voyage.

Antonia, however, did not accept his excuse. Wishing to assert her marital rights, she decided to sneak out of the house after the festivities ended and go to Menéndez in the inn where he was sleeping. She told her Spanish companion that Menéndez had summoned her to his room. An Indian maidservant accompanied them to the inn where they were admitted once the Spanish companion explained Menéndez had requested their presence. Once inside his room, Antonia tiptoed to his bed with a candle fluttering. Menéndez awoke, startled, and asked why she was there. The Spanish lady, now aware that Antonia had tricked her, stuttered an apology. With that, Menéndez laughed heartily and offered the ladies gifts of clothing and food. By all accounts, Antonia was then returned to her own bed in her host's house.

Menéndez, amused but concerned about Antonia's despondency, took her and her Indian companions with him back to her home with the Calusas. Once there, he left her in the hands of her brother Carlos and continued his mission of exploration and colonization.

As he traveled south along the Florida coast on a return trip to Havana, a storm drove the ships into a harbor near the present Florida Keys. By this time, word of Doña Antonia's "marriage" and travels had spread to nearby tribes. The Spaniards found themselves in a region inhabited by the Tequesta Indians, their chief being a distant relative of Carlos and Antonia. He told Menéndez and his men that, although his people killed all the Christians shipwrecked in his territory, he would do them no harm. His people loved Doña Antonia, the wife of the great

Adelantado, and would spare the Christians in her name. This saved the lives of the storm-tossed Spaniards, but did not stop tension mounting between other tribes, specifically Carlos' Calusas and the northern tribe of the Tocobagas to the north.

As Menéndez continued his quest for peace he was acutely aware of the dangers surrounding him. Carlos was posing more and more of a threat and the Adelantado feared for the lives of all Europeans in Florida. In April 1567, he dispatched Francisco de Reinoso, a military man of the Crown, to the Calusa Nation. By this time Carlos had chosen as heir to his throne a Christianized Indian given the name of Don Pedro. Menéndez realized Carlos was increasingly a threat to the Spanish and to the converted Indians and neighboring tribes. He was devising a plan for Don Pedro to marry Doña Antonia since both would then be heirs to Carlos' possessions and, hopefully, would continue the attempt to convert the Indians.

Although it appeared danger to the settlers was temporarily abated, nonetheless Menéndez sent Reinoso back to Havana with Antonia and her companions for their safety. Leaving the women again with the Rojas family, Reinoso immediately returned to Carlos and wrote back to Havana about the hardships and dangers they were living through. It was discovered Carlos and his father had slain more than two hundred Christians over a twenty-year period and now was threatening to kill Reinoso and other Christians unless Antonia was returned to his village. Instead of sailing back to St. Augustine, Menéndez took Antonia and her entourage back to Calusa territory. By this time it was obvious Antonia had become a pawn to be used by her own brother and the Adelantado.

Antonia was with her brother when Menéndez met with Carlos to persuade him to make peace with his enemy the Tocobaga. A peace-making agreement orchestrated by Menéndez left Carlos angry and Antonia livid. The formerly passive Indian maiden told Menéndez that, "You have two hearts. One is for yourself and the other for the Tocobaga. For me and my brother, you have none!"

The tirade continued, leaving Menéndez stunned. Was this the woman his men joked had been trained from birth to be silent? Was this the discreet and shy princess he had taken as a bride years ago?

Whatever Menéndez thought, Antonia made her point and he left the Calusa Nation to return to St. Augustine and the regions on the East Coast of Florida. There are no records to show he ever saw Antonia again. She remained a Catholic, teaching her tribesmen the religion she loved. She did, however, also maintain her loyalty to her brother.

By 1568 the Spanish could no longer tolerate Carlos' hostility.

Reinoso, whose life had been tenuous at best, was one of several soldiers who finally killed Carlos. Menéndez was heartsick at the loss of his Indian friend whom he considered a brother. Although it rid the Spanish settlers of a serious threat to their occupancy of the land, nonetheless Menéndez grieved.

Putting that chapter behind him, Menéndez strove to develop the capital of Florida in Santa Elena, a settlement he had established in 1566 near present-day Parris Island, South Carolina. In 1571, Menéndez' Spanish wife, Ana Maria, joined him there. Doña Maria arrived with servants and luxurious household goods to include leather wall hangings, beds with scarlet-fringed canopies, pewter table services, and candlestick holders. It was a bold move for the pampered wife of the Spanish hero, but she was pleased to make the adjustment that posed far fewer hardships than those experienced in the still struggling town of St. Augustine. Unfortunately, Menéndez died in Santander, Spain, in 1574 while Ana Maria was still in Santa Elena. Additionally, Santa Elena was destined to fall to Indian attacks, and by 1587 was abandoned, returning St. Augustine to its former status as capital of La Florida.

One wonders if Antonia ever knew about the real Señora Menéndez, or if the Señora ever knew about Antonia. Certainly Antonia would have been distressed to know what luxuries Doña Maria was given in life compared to that with which she lived. Or perhaps, in the end, Antonia was happy with what she had achieved for herself and her people. Her dual role as the "wife" of the Adelantado and a much loved Native American gave her reason to be proud.

The story of Antonia was creatively depicted as the character of Princess Notina in Florida's official state play *Cross and Sword*. Author Paul Green, noted for his historic outdoor dramas including North Carolina's *The Lost Colony*, *Texas*, and *The Stephen Foster Story*, developed the character of the brave and beautiful Notina on stage. For over thirty years the public saw the lovely and alluring Notina (named as an anagram of "Antonia") as a heroine helping Menéndez establish the budding settlement of St. Augustine where she met and fell in love with Menéndez. It is she who personifies the Indian Calusa princess who, in reality, never saw St. Augustine, but did indeed give her hand in "marriage" to the powerful Spanish leader.

Antonia of history wasn't beautiful—brave, certainly—but not attractive. She gracefully accepted her destiny and controlled it whenever possible. Her life was full of twists and turns, but she chose her way carefully and she knew her own mind. Menéndez was no match for the complex woman. Although Antonia remained for a time with her Calusa tribesmen after Menéndez' final departure, she did return to Havana where she died some years later.

Antonia, indeed, became one of the first women in what is now the continental United States to have her name written beside those of the men making history as the New World was slowly developing. She depicts one of the first daring daughters.[2]

☙

DOÑA SEBASTIANA CENDOYA
Against All Odds (1670s)

The story of Doña Sebastiana is a tale that transcends borders and centuries. A pregnant woman with two young children loses her husband suddenly. Before she has time to grieve, government officials ignore her needs and demand a complete inventory of her husband's possessions and claim she owes them money. Alone in an unfamiliar land far from home, she is left to the mercies of men in positions as high as the Spanish Crown. She is forced to fight for her rights. The implications of Doña Sebastiana Olazarrage y Aramburu's story surpass her own unfortunate circumstances.

Doña Sebastiana was married to Sergeant Major Manuel de Cendoya. The couple and their two babies, one a toddler, the other an infant, arrived in St. Augustine on July 6, 1671. Queen Regent Mariana of Spain had appointed Cendoya governor of La Florida, charging him with the responsibility of overseeing the construction of a new masonry fort. It was a position of high responsibility and the twenty-two-year veteran of service to the crown felt honored to accept the position.

Leaving Cadiz, Spain, in July 1670, the governor and his family went first to Mexico City where, for nine months, Cendoya presented his views for fortification of Florida and haggled with the Viceroy, the Marquess de Mancera, about funding for the monumental project.

His stay in Mexico City later became a source of contention between the Cendoya family and the officials in Spain. On October 1, 1671, Cendoya petitioned Queen Mariana for his salary during the year after his departure from Cadiz and his arrival in Mexico. He also asked for salary for his young son who he had enlisted as a private in the military. (Regardless of age, this was a common practice at the time.) This petition would later be a major obstacle for the young widow Sebastiana to overcome.

Within a month of the family's arrival in St. Augustine, one year

The construction of the Castillo de San Marcos was under the charge of Governor Manuel Cendoya, whose wife Doña Sebastiana was forced to fight for her life after the governor's death in St. Augustine. (Photo courtesy of the National Park Service)

after leaving Spain, workmen began drawing pay and the lengthy preparations of choosing a site and obtaining building material began. Groundbreaking took place on October 2, 1672, with Cendoya officiating in the first formal gathering for the fort, designated as the Castillo de San Marcos. He later laid the first stone and when labor was short, he often worked alongside the Indians while ordering his soldiers to participate in the digging of the foundation trench.

As work progressed, he realized how labor intensive the project was and frequently appealed for more money for wages or for more workers. Meanwhile, his petition for his salary and a salary for his son was turned down. The recommendation to disapprove the petition stated Cendoya had not justified his stop in Mexico.

Although the petition was denied in February 7, 1673, it is doubtful he ever knew of the rejection. The governor died March 8, 1673, one month and one day later.

He was buried the same day of his death and before Doña Sebastiana could close the doors of her home to begin grieving, the royal officials entered Government House. Acting Governor Nicolás Ponce de León demanded an inventory and attachment of the estate of the deceased governor, claiming he was in debt to the royal treasury for 16,000 pesos.

For two days Doña Sebastiana was subjected to the invasion of her home as the men listed every item she owned. When they finished, they made her take an oath stating the entire estate had been listed on the inventory. With her wits about her, the widow said the entire estate was listed but her claim to the Crown took priority by virtue of her marriage contract and her dowry. She made it clear she would fight for her rights, and fight she did.

With no funds, the young mother continued to care for her children. Her third child, born in April, exacerbated her desperate situation. Soon after the baby's birth she wrote to the Crown for relief. She said the "small amount of money paid to her husband as a salary had been deposited in the royal *exchequer* so the artisans on the construction could be paid and the work could be continued."

With no response, she again implored the Crown to assist her financially, explaining she was alone with three children and no funds to return to her homeland. She said her late husband's trip to Mexico was necessary and the Crown owed them money for the twenty months he served as governor. She begged officials to send her the amount needed for passage for herself and her dependents. In her communications she explained the inventory of her husband's property included family jewels, her bed, and her clothing. She had nothing, and no way to leave for Spain. The young widow was destitute.

The issue of the stop in Mexico was difficult at best, but a further complication arose when it was discovered that Cendoya had ordered merchandise from Havana which did not reach St. Augustine until after Doña Sebastiana's July petition. Her oath that the March inventory was complete and no other property was outstanding was therefore contested. The estate also included the materials sent from Havana. With this, the widow again appealed to the Crown, explaining that the death of her husband created numerous financial obligations and she and her children desperately needed to return to Spain.

As a woman of rank, Doña Sebastiana finally drew the attention of Viceroy Marquess de Mancera of Nueva España. He responded to a letter from her and "remarked to the queen that the services of the late governor, the infancy of his children, and the privations and obligations which had befallen his widow were grounds for equity and justice. He hoped that Doña Sebastiana and her children were worthy of the royal charity."

The response from Mancera's request left Doña Sebastiana the victim of a cruel hoax. A recommendation was made that the widow be awarded two thousand ducats for return transportation, collectible in Mexico. However, the amount she actually would receive included the accrued unpaid salary and the amounts furnished from her own pocket to pay for the fortification work. Transportation funds and money she claimed the Crown owed her were lumped into one payment of two thousand ducats.

Nonetheless, she did attempt to collect the money offered her. Unfortunately, she continued to lose to the crafty bureaucrats who dodged her pleas, and her debts mounted as she fought for her life and the welfare of her children. After six years elapsed the attachment of 16,000 pesos had not been lifted and the estate amounting to approximately 3,000 pesos balanced the debt of 3,000 pesos incurred by Doña Sebastiana over the years.

Although letters from officials continued to explain her destitute circumstances, the Crown did nothing to help her.

Finally, in 1681, Governor Juan Márquez reviewed the matter and took a different approach. He listed four charges against the deceased which included failure to visit the provinces, establishment of a dry goods store, establishment of certain fees to be used by himself and other officials, and the appointment of twenty-four individuals to the rank of officer. He then acquitted Cendoya of the first charge and fined the estate an amount equal to about $5.00 or $6.00 in present-day American currency. The fourth charge was referred to the *Consejo de Indias,* a Spanish government office.

In sending his report to the Crown, he praised Governor Cendoya and pleaded for Doña Sebastiana. He explained that she had been "detained in St. Augustine for eight years and the charity of the residents had supported her in gratefulness for the exemplary actions of her husband."

In 1682 the *Consejo* exonerated Cendoya on all charges. Over the next few months arguments ensued over the exact amounts owed to the widow. Eventually she collected some of the money, but certainly nothing to compensate her grief and tribulations.

Ten years after the demise of Governor Cendoya, the case was closed. If Doña Sebastiana collected her due in person, she would still have been in St. Augustine. Nothing is known of her after that point. She and her children simply disappear from historical accounts.

Historian and author Luis Arana who wrote of Cendoya and his widow in the *El Escribano* articles summed up the worth of the ten years of anguish endured by Doña Sebastiana. He said, "(Her) tribulations in St. Augustine were not in vain because eventually they contributed to the welfare of her fellow women." She diligently tried to fight her own fight but her appeals for justice fell on deaf ears. Finally with the support of men in high positions, particularly Governor Márquez, her situation was finally reviewed.

The result of the ten years of anguish was sweet relief. In 1685 Spain decreed that the wives of deceased governors of Florida could return to Spain without the estate being settled. This was of no benefit to Doña Sebastiana, nor would it help wives other than those of the governors. If nothing else, however, it was a step forward and a certain victory for Doña Sebastiana, despite or because of her travails.

≈

MANUELA DE MIER MICKLER
Minorcan Matriarch (1790s–1870)

Hearing the name Manuela de Mier Mickler generally elicits a smile from those who know about her. She is, after all, somewhat of a legend as the Mickler mother of fifteen, a poker-playing Minorcan mom, and a southern sympathizer who sent a Yankee husband packing, thus earning the tongue-in-cheek nickname of "Grandma Dove."

So who was this Minorcan marvel? She was born in the age when Florida was just waking to the dawn of Americanization.

Manuela de Jesus Hilaria de Mier Mickler was born into the third generation of Minorcans who came to Florida in 1768 and remained throughout the changing governments of the eighteenth and nineteenth centuries.

It was Manuela's grandfather, Lazaro de Ortega, who was brought to Florida as a boy of thirteen with 1,255 immigrants to the mosquito-infested shores of New Smyrna.[1] The immigrants were indentured servants enticed from the Balearic island of Minorca off the coast of Spain and from Greece, Italy, and Corsica. They were gathered by Dr. Andrew Turnbull to work on his indigo plantations with a promise of land in payment for labor. It was a promise never kept.

Lazaro was twenty-two in 1777 when the settlers fled from New Smyrna to St. Augustine to seek sanctuary. The homeless refugees began a new life in British-ruled St. Augustine, forming new family groups and mingling together in newfound freedom.

Lazaro married Minorcan native Catalina Lleres in 1781. Lazaro and Catalina probably knew each other during the difficult years in New Smyrna, but that relationship can only be surmised. Their lives as man

Manuela de Mier Mickler, the feisty "Minorcan Mama," is a favorite of the legendary Minorcan figures. (Photo courtesy of Latrell E. Mickler)

and wife began two years before the end of the British twenty-year occupation and the return of the Spanish to Florida. The Minorcans were relieved when Florida was restored to Spanish rule and inhabited by people who spoke the native tongue of the majority of the settlers. They also were pleased to be in a community dominated by the Catholic faith of their upbringing rather than the unfamiliar Protestant beliefs of the British Anglicans.

Lazaro and Catalina's daughter, Ana Margarita de Ortega, was born December 1, 1789, and grew up during the years of Spanish occupation ending in 1821. One of the Spaniards who arrived in St. Augustine during that time period was Antonio José Fernando de Mier from Cadiz,

Spain. Antonio met Ana Margarita and they soon married.

During the years of Spanish rule, Antonio and Ana's family increased with the addition of four children, one of whom was Manuela. Her birth in 1816 came during the final years of European occupation before United States ownership.

Although Manuela was born into a Spanish community to Spanish parents, English was a familiar language to her and her parents. Minorca, the homeland of Manuela's grandparents, had been granted to Great Britain by the terms of the Treaty of Paris of 1763, the treaty also giving Britain control of Florida. In addition, it was not unusual for Englishmen from the former British colonies to migrate to Florida. And so it was with the Mickler family. The Micklers (pronounced Mike-ler) were descendants of Palatine Germans who emigrated from Europe to the New World in the 1700s. The branch of the family finding its way to Florida came down from South Carolina with Robert Mickler, the first known Mickler to arrive.

Robert, born in 1800, came to St. Augustine around 1814, two years before the birth of Manuela. He went to work for Manuela's father, probably helping cultivate the land acquired by Antonio through a Spanish grant. Robert was well established in St. Augustine when Manuel's father, Antonio de Mier, died in 1823. Evidently Robert was very close to the family as he married the widow Ana in 1825 when he was twenty-five and she ten years his senior. They had three children adding to the family of Ana's four offspring of which Manuela was one.

Manuela was fifteen in 1831 when she married Robert's first cousin twenty-eight-year-old Jacob Mickler, thus further tightening the ties that bind the Minorcans and Micklers. Ana and Robert's three children were cousins to the fifteen offspring of Manuela and Jacob as well as being half-brothers of Manuela.

Those are the facts, the rest is as much myth as reality. It is documented that Manuela de Mier Mickler gave birth to fifteen children, ten of whom lived to maturity. The births are documented, but legends are made by productive women like that and stories abound. An article in the *St. Augustine Record* on March 20, 1940, ran a headline saying, "Micklers were "Good Fighters" and "Good Lovers." Considering the fact that the youngest child, Catherine, was born just after Jacob's death makes one wonder. Was Manuela too much for him? The article refers to her as "that redoubtable woman who reared 15 children. . . ."

Two sets of twins were included in the count of children. One sibling in each set died in infancy. A list compiled by Mickler descendants records births almost every even-numbered year from 1832 until

1856 missing only 1848.[2] The exceptions to the even-numbered years were Joseph born in 1853 who died in infancy and baby Catherine born in 1857 ending the long line of children.

Of the six adult sons produced by Manuela and Jacob, five fought for the Confederacy during the Civil War. Yulee, born in 1850, was too young to serve. Concrete evidence of Manuela's contribution to the war effort can be found in inscriptions on the Confederate War Memorial in the Plaza de la Constitución. Antonio, George, and Jacob Mickler are commemorated with other St. Augustine sons who died fighting during the Civil War. Two other sons entered the army but survived their service for the South. One, William Felix, served during Seminole Indian War skirmishes before joining the Confederate Army. He was elected to the Florida legislature in 1860 and was a member when the ordinance of secession was adopted.

Another son, Robert, joined the Confederate Army at age fifteen and returned to become a railroad conductor and pilot commissioner at Mayport and Jacksonville, Florida.

The deed that keeps Manuela's name popping up like a wildflower in the crop of Minorcan and Mickler stories is her marriage after the Civil War to a Massachusetts Yankee known as Captain Dove. This is the stuff that legends are made of. After sending five sons off to war to uphold the South's position and losing three of them, how could this dear widow woman marry a Yankee? Folklore said the children couldn't stomach a Yankee in their midst and Manuela sent him back up north with no second thoughts. One can only guess the reasons for his departure from St. Augustine. We will never know for sure. With a constitution as strong as Manuela's, it is doubtful she would have bowed to any pressure from her children. She probably decided he simply didn't fit her Southern lifestyle.

The name stuck, however, and she became known as "Grandma Dove." It would seem the name was applied in jest. Why would she, the Mickler mother of fifteen children—ten surviving to adulthood—keep the name of a man whose first name isn't recorded anywhere in family records and whose identity other than "a Captain from Massachusetts" remains a mystery? "Dove" doesn't seem an appropriate appellation for the little lady who probably was anything but the peaceful image elicited by the name.

The stories about Manuela continue. Descendant Latrell E. Mickler, author of *Indigo*, a novel involving the plight and ultimate escape of the Minorcans in New Smyrna, said Manuela was known to be an avid card player. Some say she loved poker. Whether poker or something more benign, she was known for keeping a deck of playing cards close at hand. Patricia Ferguson Mickler wrote in *The Micklers of Florida*, "Manuela had a devotion to cards and she is known to have carried her own pack of cards with her."

An *El Escribano* article about Jacob Mickler certainly corroborates the card-playing stories. It seems Mama Manuela passed down the card-playing prowess to her son. Authors David J. Coles and Zack C. Waters describe Jacob Mickler as demonstrating a "unique, colorful personality" quoting an authority as saying Mickler was "an excellent card player and sent all of his winnings to his mother in St. Augustine."[3]

So, here we have Manuela Mickler, the Minorcan mama. Manuela forever united the Minorcans with the Micklers, even more than her mother Ana, who married the first Mickler in Florida. Manuela's daughters, Margaret and Manuela II, married first cousins John and William Mickler, continuing the pattern of intermarriage. Who would have guessed the branches of that family tree would become inextricably entwined, but they did.

The card-playing, multiple-mother, Southern sympathizer called "Grandma Dove" will be remembered fondly in family lore and St. Augustine history.

CHAPTER II

Women in Danger

❧

MARIA ANDREU
The Lady of the Light (1854–1862)

Lighthouses are perceived to be romantic and idyllic: the strong beam caressing the darkness; the welcome brightness penetrating the fog; the glimpse of a tall tower beckoning to safe shores.

But Maria Andreu didn't fantasize about life near a lighthouse—she lived it. She knew firsthand the hard work and the danger that befell lighthouse keepers. She was one of the "ladies of the light." Records of the early female lamplighters are scarce but women were known to assume the difficult duty of keeping the lanterns lit. Usually they worked alongside their husbands or fathers, and it was not unusual to see them officially appointed as keeper after the death or illness of the man in charge. Maria was one who followed that difficult path.

Maria Andreu was born Maria de los Delores Mestre on April 25, 1801. She and Joseph Andreu, whom she married in 1822, were both of Minorcan descent. Their lineage was through the group of Mediterranean settlers who emigrated to St. Augustine from New Smyrna, Florida, in 1777. Maria and Joseph were born during Spanish rule of Florida and married the year after Florida became a United States territory in 1821.

Maria was well aware of the watchtower that was to become Florida's first official lighthouse. Wooden watchtowers had existed off the coast of St. Augustine from the time Don Pedro Menéndez claimed Florida for Spain in 1565. The general location for a tower was on the northeast end of Anastasia Island, a narrow eighteen-mile strip of land running south from the St. Augustine inlet. Over the years a variety of towers provided a lookout station for sentries and a warning signal about the sandy shoals threatening sea traffic.

The stone tower that stood on Anastasia Island when the Americans came was sadly in need of repair. Originally constructed in the 1700s, it had been used by the British and then again by the Spanish who, knowing their hold on Florida was tenuous at best, had little need to maintain the post.

In 1823 the United States Government officially lit the light and appointed Juan Andreu, uncle of Joseph, as the first American keeper. By the time Joseph was installed as keeper in 1854, he and Maria had become well acquainted with the lighthouse through numerous visits with Juan.

Maria was mother to eight children born between 1822 and 1846, all with names of Spanish derivation: Margarita Maria a las Nieves Matilda, Epfenia, Genoveva, Idelfensa, Martina, Guilluma, Florence, and Nicholas. Of those eight the five oldest were married by the time Joseph became keeper. Guilluma, Florence, and Nicholas were twelve, ten, and eight respectively.

The keeper's life was difficult though not unpleasant. Lighthouse tending was a governmentally controlled job, which meant supplies were provided for maintenance of the light and some subsistence. For food it was necessary to grow fruits and vegetables and to fish and hunt.

The St. Augustine Lighthouse complex looked much like this in the 1850s and 1860s when Maria Andreu lived and worked there.

Housekeeping duties, including the children's education, were all done by the keeper's wife, in this case Maria.

Maintaining the light included the strenuous work of climbing the tower to change the oil. By 1855 whale oil was replaced by lard oil facilitating the task somewhat by reducing the weight of the fuel and producing a cleaner burn. Even with that welcome change the wicks still needed to be trimmed and the light watched continuously throughout the night. No doubt Maria and even the children shared the strenuous tasks as they were able.

It was in early December 1859 that Maria witnessed the shocking death of her husband. While attempting to whitewash the sixty-foot tower, the lashing of the scaffold gave way and Joseph plunged to the ground. *The St. Augustine Examiner* of December 10, 1859, reported the dramatic incident graphically explaining that he first struck the roof of the oil room thirty feet below the top, then glanced off the stone wall and landed on the pavement of the ground below. His death from a broken neck was instantaneous and left Maria suddenly a widow with three children and no income. It did not take her long to realize that despite the difficulties, remaining at the light station as keeper would provide her the best source of livelihood. On December 29, 1859, Maria was appointed keeper. She was granted the full $400.00 per year salary, a tribute to her since women frequently were not given payment equal to that of men.

The Examiner reported the appointment on January 7, 1860, applauding the decision with a somewhat backhanded compliment, "We are sure that this appointment will commend itself to all as a fast and kind recognition of the services of her much respected deceased husband and as a just provision for the support of a poor and deserving widow who has been deprived of her stay and support. . . ."

A local storyteller tells of Maria's distress at the time of her husband's death. In the tale Maria climbs the tower asking for guidance in determining her future. She is answered by her dead husband's voice telling her to "Tend the Light." She followed the instructions and remained at the lighthouse complex.

One drawback for Maria was her lack of physical strength. She could not carry the heavy buckets up the tower nor repair the heavy equipment. Help came from Assistant Keeper Joseph Mickler. Maria, however, maintained primary care of the facility as she continued her chores as housekeeper and mother. Life as a keeper required constant watch of the light throughout the night and daily entries into the government log books. Inspections were yearly and often unexpected. It was not a leisurely life.

Maria managed her responsibilities until war encroached upon the little community of St. Augustine. The town had mixed sentiments for both North and South. Although the town was regionally located in the South, many citizens considered themselves Northerners. The first battle cry came from leaders championing the Southern cause. Confederate Army Colonel George Couper Gibbs ordered the light extinguished. Fearing the coastal light would aid the Union Navy he dismantled the lens and hid it. He and his men continued the practice dimming other lights along the Florida eastern shore.

Without the light there was no pay for Maria and she was left vulnerable on her little island compound with nowhere to turn. Additionally, the encroachment of the ocean made the compound more and more vulnerable to the fierce Nor'easters that swept the coast. And without the light as a beacon the dangerous shoals once again posed a threat to passing ships.

Maria managed to stay on the compound until 1862 when, at age sixty-one, she quietly slipped out of St. Augustine. It is believed she spent her last years with a daughter in Georgia; however, no documentation of her destination is available.

The lamp of the lighthouse Maria served was relit in 1867. The beam swept across the beaches until the new tower was completed in 1874. In later years a second woman took over the duties of keeper. Kay Harn assumed responsibility for the light when her husband William died in 1889. Maria, however, was the only woman to serve Florida's first official lighthouse.

The St. Augustine Lighthouse continues to serves as a navigational aid.

᭓

LOLA SANCHEZ

Espionage on Horseback (Civil War Years)

No military battles were fought in or near St. Augustine during the Civil War, but the conflict had a significant impact on the town and its environs. One famous war story is the tale of the ride of Mary Dolores "Lola" Sanchez. Lola and her family, descendants of Spaniards from the First Spanish Period, lived in a little country farmhouse located on the east side of the St. Johns River near Palatka.

Although some details of her daring deed vary, her adventure is

described in *The Branches: Springs of Living Water*, a booklet commemo-
rating the centennial of a county parish of the Catholic church in St.
Johns County.

Lola and her sisters were Confederate sympathizers, well aware of
the presence of Union forces nearby. As with many people of that time
they maintained friendly relations with the enemy for protection and
sometimes surveillance. One night the sisters were alone when an opportunity arose to entertain the soldiers in blue. As the young women prepared supper, they overheard the soldiers discussing plans to commandeer
supplies from neighboring farms. The soldiers also indiscreetly mentioned
a planned attack on a Confederate camp along the St. Johns River. Hearing this Lola decided to alert the Confederate troops to the impending
danger. In order to depart unnoticed the sisters decided to prolong dinner preparations while Lola made what can be considered today a Paul
Revere ride of warning.

Saddling a horse, Lola rode in the direction of the Confederate
camp. It is at this point the story varies. Most versions of the legend

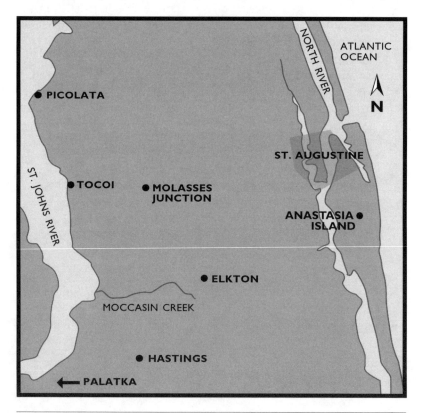

describe her leaving her horse and rowing across the St. Johns River. Other observations lead to the conclusion that she could not have crossed the St. Johns River and returned home in the time allotted without her absence being detected by the soldiers.

A survey of the area offers possible alternatives of rowing north or south along the river bank to the camp or riding to Moccasin Creek and crossing there. Since the location of the camp is unknown and the site of the farm only speculative, it is hard to say exactly where Lola Sanchez crossed the creek or river.

She did, however, manage to ride to a body of water, row across, ride a borrowed horse to the Confederate camp, and relay information to the soldiers. All this was accomplished in enough time for her to return home and sit down with the soldiers to a pleasant supper cooked by her sisters.

Lola's story also has a twist regarding her father. One version states he was not home that night because he was held prisoner by the Union soldiers. A second version tells of his capture after Lola's flight and his imprisonment then. It is said he was incarcerated at Fort Marion, the current Castillo de San Marcos, because Union soldiers believed he had imparted information to the Confederates. Either way, it is known he was a prisoner of war at the fort.

The details of Lola's ride will never be verified. The fact that she accomplished the courageous feat is part of St. Augustine's folklore and credit is given to the brave young woman who rode through the night for the sake of her Confederate compatriots.[1]

✦

KAT TWINE
Civil Rights Imprisonment (1960s)

She kept her bags packed back in 1964. She had to. She never knew when she might be thrown into jail.

Katherine A. Twine—known to everyone as "Kat"—was as generous with hugs as she was with home-baked cakes and cookies. She was not your average crusader but that was the role she played as a black woman of the 1960s.

Kat couldn't eat in the restaurants in town. She could shop at the local Woolworth's on King Street and McCrory's on St. George Street but she couldn't stop for a coke. She explained, "The women who worked there would call me up to tell me that my thread was in—I used to crochet—and I could spend money there. I could buy anything but a drink."[1]

Woolworth's was the scene of St. Augustine's first sit-in during the civil rights struggles. Kat remembered when young Henry Thomas made his mark by being the first black to demand service at the Woolworth lunch counter.

"They didn't know what to do with him so they turned the lights out at the lunch counter and called the sheriff. They arrested the boy and put him in jail. Later they let him out but they tried to claim he was crazy so they could send him to Chattahoochie (one of the state mental institutions). But he screamed and yelled and raised so much cane they decided not to do that—so they put him back in jail again."

Kat was brought up to believe in herself. Her father's nickname for her was "Somebody" and she blossomed with pride and self-confidence. When she was young she questioned why the colored kids didn't ride school buses like the white kids. She knew something was wrong, but it wasn't until she was a wife and a mother of her own child that she found the opportunity to act on her beliefs—and she did.

Kat Twine was the first adult arrested in St. Augustine during the years of civil strife. The arrests of protesting students from the Murray High School, the colored secondary facility, preceded hers and she soon became jailmates with them. She said she always had her own bed because the "children," as she called them, said she snored. Whatever the reason she was sure of a bed to sleep on during the four times she was arrested. Food, though, was another matter. She never ate the jail food. She said they used to slide a metal tray of food under the door but she wouldn't eat it.

"There was a 6-inch gap under the door and they pushed the food under it like we were animals. They didn't have the decency to open the door. I wouldn't touch that food. I don't even know what was on the trays." She does admit to cajoling a prison trustee into bringing her cookies from the commissary.

Was Kat really a brave, strong-willed protester? Absolutely. Her courage was demonstrated in actions flowing from a strength fear could not subdue. Yes, she was scared. She talked about a nighttime meeting of the blacks and the Ku Klux Klan. The blacks left St. Mary's Church in Lincolnville and walked together toward the downtown plaza singing and praying. It was crowded with Klansmen, some hooded, some not. She said, "I felt a chill. Like the hair raising on the back of my neck. I knew something was going to happen."

It did.

*Kat Twine is radiant in January 2002 during a cere-
mony for the dedication of the Great Floridian Award
marker in honor of her late husband Henry Twine.
(Photo by Karen Harvey)*

C. T. Vivian, a deputy of Dr. Martin Luther King Jr., fell to his knees in prayer. The Klansmen beat him and kicked him as the police stood by silently. The police dogs started barking as Kat and her friends watched helplessly. She believed they were going to kill him. It was then she found her strength.

"All of a sudden I wasn't scared anymore, because I knew I was doing the right thing. We were doing what we had to do."

As the summer of 1964 heated up, blacks and whites alike became fearful of the action that was slipping out of control. Some of Kat's friends were told to stay away from her as she adamantly moved forth with determination. She believed that the women would not be injured, yet the door was open for trouble. She described an incident that both shook her and strengthened her.

"During one protest there was a young white man with me from New England who carried his Bible with him to pray. He held it up in front of him. They would take the cattle prod and they would stick him with it. I was the oldest woman out there. I never let those children know that I was scared. I had to stay strong for them."

Kat's sense of duty was reflected in her loyalty to her family. On Mother's Day 1964 the police made a night raid on the Twine house. Nighttime arrests were a common practice and Kat hated it. This time she had enough and she wanted to spend Mother's Day with her mother so she hid from the police. After she and her mother celebrated the day together Kat dutifully turned herself in to the police and was promptly put back in a cell.

Her husband Henry was doing his part. Henry was president of the local NAACP and later the Southern Christian Leadership Coalition. He was in constant contact with civil rights leaders outside the community. Both Henry and Kat were among those who made the initial contacts with Dr. King in 1963 leading to the sultry summer of 1964 protests. He was never arrested however. Kat believes he might have been spared incarceration because he was a postal worker and therefore a government employee. She doesn't know that for sure. She does know, however, that his work to gain blacks their rights raised the respect of the community. Henry went on to become the first black vice-mayor of St. Augustine and although he was defeated, he made a commendable effort in a race for the mayoral position. He served almost ten years as a city commissioner.

Both Kat and Henry wanted life to be much easier for their son Teddy, who was four years old in 1964. Recalling her years growing up with segregation she said, "I didn't want my four-year-old son, Teddy to grow up that way. I didn't want him to be treated the way I was treated."

Kat was also a mainstay of support for her sister Jean, who was also arrested several times. On one occasion the guards had walked all the prisoners outside into the yard on a very hot day when Jean was overcome by the heat and fainted. Kat told the tale.

"The jailer's wife, Mrs. Cook, and I went to help her. We were trying to get her up when a man pointed a shotgun at me and said, 'You're not going anyplace.'"

Kat responded, "You better go ahead and shoot me, cause I ain't leaving my sister." Mrs. Cook knew Kat from work in the hospital where Kat was a nurse and intervened telling the man to let Kat be with her sister. The man lowered his gun and stepped aside.

Kat talked about the time one hundred blacks were arrested during a protest. She said it was crowded, but they made the most of it. They talked and sang and she said, "I did some crocheting." She did indeed make the best of it.

In June of 2001 the city of St. Augustine bestowed the highest local honor possible on Katherine "Kat" Twine—the Aviles Civic Recognition of Public Service Award in gratitude for service to the people of St. Augustine. The irony of receiving the prestigious award was not lost on Kat who accepted it with her usual dignity.[2]

Kat might laugh today about some of the incidents. Certainly when her husband Henry was alive they both shared the humor of the situation. They particularly loved the story of the invasion of the Monson Motel swimming pool, a motel strategically placed on the well-traveled bayfront. A group of spirited rabbis and a few young black women jumped into the segregated pool. The police arrived and jumped in after them, which just added to the confusion. The motel owner poured muriatic acid into the pool, but that didn't quell their spirits. When the uninvited swimmers finally left, the determined segregationists put a full-grown alligator in the pool. The last laugh was on those who lugged the alligator to the pool. The demonstrators had already moved the action out of town and onto the beach.

Although it was a difficult time for Kat Twine, she never stopped passing out hugs and cookies and always kept on crocheting. Kat took a solid stand for her beliefs and her actions made a difference.

CHAPTER III

Overcoming Adversity

✤

MARY EVANS
Maria of the Oldest House (1784–1792)

In 1977 Eugenia Price published a novel called *Maria*. It is a classic romantic tale about a beautiful woman and the men involved in her achievements and failures in life. In it a woman of the eighteenth century battles numerous hardships in St. Augustine during the turbulent times of the ebb and flow of British and Spanish occupation. The book quickly gained popularity with readers of romance novels, historic stories, and tales of valiant women.

Because of the book, Maria—born Mary Evans in South Carolina in 1730—is probably the most recognizable of all the "Daring Daughters" documented here. Tourists to the town visit "The Oldest House" where Maria lived and ask in awe, "Is this really Maria's house?" Men in tour groups laugh when tour guides comment on Maria's third marriage. "She was very clever . . . she married a man half her age."

Indeed Mary Evans did live in the house and yes, her third husband was half her age. He was twenty-eight and she fifty-six when they married—and she outlived him by fifteen months.

For more than those reasons, Mary Evans deserves attention beyond that of a romantic heroine. Her arrival in St. Augustine in 1763 was a time of turmoil as the Spanish left Florida just short of two centuries of occupation. Her expertise as a midwife gave her almost immediate respectability and prestige and her ability to purchase and manage property brought her increasing status over the years.

Her first husband "David" Fenwick[1] died very early during the British years and Mary remarried Joseph Peavett, a British military man. Peavett held the rank of sergeant at the time, later leaving the military to engage in business pursuits. By 1781 his increased wealth earned him a position in the lower house of the General Assembly of East Florida. At some point he joined the Florida militia providing him with the rank of Captain.[2]

It was during her marriage to Peavett that Mary became the mistress of the St. Francis Street dwelling now called the "Oldest House."★ During the time the couple owned the house they added the second floor, put in window panes, a fireplace, and most importantly established a tavern in the house. The tavern, which Mary helped manage, was a serendipitous afterthought, but with which Mary was most agreeable. Since the house was across the street from the St. Francis Barracks, it provided a perfect gathering spot for the soldiers after receiving their paychecks.

The former Franciscan Monastery was renovated as military barracks during the British period. According to Price, it was also a place for whispered discussions about loyalties held in the British province during the time of the American Revolution. This is one of the intriguing aspects of both the book *Maria* and the life of Mary Evans. If Mary, from South Carolina, had any leanings toward independence from the British Crown, she kept her feelings to herself by remaining loyal to the British. She knew of the rebellious activities in the colonies, but Florida was destined to remain loyal to the Crown and she could not endanger her standing in the British colony.

During the British decades (1763–1784), Mary and Joseph both grew in prominence purchasing land, slaves, and livestock. At the end of the British Period they owned 2,110 acres, a house and property in St. Augustine, fifty-seven slaves, a white servant, four horses, one cow, and three calves.[3]

The Peavetts' status was substantial when Florida was once again turned over to the Spanish. They elected to remain in the Spanish-held territory and Mary was firmly established in St. Augustine when Joseph died in 1786.

It was here that Mary exhibited a tragic flaw. As a wealthy woman of fifty-six, she married young John Hudson, a twenty-eight-year-old penniless Irishman with a penchant for drinking and gambling.

★The official name of the National Historic Landmark known as the Oldest House is the Gonzáles-Alvarez House. The history of the building dates back to the early 1700s with archeological evidence supporting occupation of the site from the early 1600s. It stands today as a reminder of St. Augustine's unique history throughout changes in ownership and serves as a teaching tool for building styles and techniques in St. Augustine.

Hudson gambled away almost all of Mary's wealth and caused their exile from the city due to unpaid debts and insolent actions expressed toward the officials. It is said when he read an edict posted in the plaza ordering all foreign residents to swear allegiance to Spain, he tore down the paper and wiped his buttocks with it as an obscene gesture of defiance. He was jailed in the Castillo de San Marcos for a month. After serving the sentence he was banished from St. Augustine and both Hudson and Mary spent their last days on land owned by Mary twenty miles north of the city between the Guana and North Rivers.

Although her last years were unpleasant, Mary did not die penniless or alone. Friends, including the Catholic priest Father Thomas Hassett, Dr. Thomas Travers, and Gerardo Forrester, were with her at her death. British businessman John Leslie and landowner Juan Fatio were the executives of her will. Her foster son John Edward Tate, who inherited the land named New Waterford, was always by her side. In addition to prop-

Maria's home, now the Gonzalez-Alvarez House or "Oldest House," is open to the public. (Sketch by Jean Light Willis)

erty Mary left an estate that included luxurious household items, clothing, an extensive library, and numerous slaves.

Mary Evans' significance lies not only in her tenacity and business acumen but in her longevity. The "Oldest House" and *Maria*, the novel by Eugenia Price, gave her a life that will persist, hopefully, as long as the structure in which she lived.

Price was touched by Maria's story. She said, "In five minutes, at lunch one day during a trip to the oldest city, Eugenia Arana 'gave' me Maria. Something nearly chemical occurs in an author's mind when the *right* story comes along."[4]

Her life, as penned by Price, is a tale of stoic determination. The historic basis for the story written by Patricia C. Griffin provides substance for the novel. Mary Evans—Maria—was an unusual woman who deserves credit for rising to the top despite disruptive politics stirring up the little settlement of St. Augustine. The death of two husbands strengthened her and the disloyalty of the third did not destroy her.

Griffin noted, "Mary Evans lived a full and eventful life. She used her medical knowledge to serve the women of the town (as a midwife), added grace to the lives of three husbands, lived through the turbulent times of East Florida under two crowns, and, we would like to believe, faced the considerable vicissitudes of her own life with equanimity."[5]

Mary Evans' story encompasses a significant slice of American history as lived by a very capable woman.

❧

ANNA KINGSLEY
Embracing Freedom (1806–1870)

Anta Majigeen Njaay did not hear the approaching Kajoor warriors until shouts and screams and charging horses' hoof beats roused her that early morning in April 1806.[1] Raiders sent by the king of Kajoor rode across the West African country of Senegal with a target of the village of Jolof where Anta and her family lived. The warriors' mission was to raid and plunder the village and capture the inhabitants to be sold as slaves.

That April day Anta saw her father killed and her village burned as she was marched yoked and shackled in a long line of prisoners. That day she not only lost her freedom and her home, but also her dignity and her youth.

A young teenager when captured, Anta had grown up in a privileged class. Her ancestors came from the founders of the Jolof Empire and she had inherited the famous Njaay name traced back to the legendary Jolof ruler. Now none of that mattered. She was marched alongside the slaves of her father and her uncles on a horrendous journey to the Danish ship *Sally*, eventually ending in Havana, Cuba, where she and the others would be sold.

Having survived the rigors of the trip, her next challenge was to bring a high price and hopefully to be purchased by a kind master. Her tall, dark beauty did not betray her. She immediately caught the attention of slave trader and plantation owner Zephaniah Kingsley Jr. when she was offered for sale. Kingsley was British born but raised in Charleston, South Carolina. He had moved from a home in Nova Scotia, Canada, to occupancies in Haiti and St. Thomas, Virgin Islands.[2] He owned a plantation in Spanish East Florida when he purchased Anta and took her with him to his home. According to Daniel L. Schafer's book *Anna Kingsley,* between the time of her purchase in September 1806 and the voyage to Florida in early October, Anta and Kingsley were married in a ceremony that was "celebrated and solemnized by her native African custom. . . ."

Kingsley changed Anta's name to Anna and she became known as Anna Madgigine Jai Kingsley. Kingsley never wavered from asserting she was his wife and their mulatto children his own.

Anna's first glimpse of Florida was when the schooner *Esther* docked in St. Augustine in order for Kingsley to register Anna and two African women he had purchased as residents of the province. From there they sailed up the St. Johns River for forty miles ending the trip at Doctor's Lake on the west shore of the river. This was Kingsley's land and Anna's first home away from Africa.

The day Anna set foot on the plantation called Laurel Grove, she was immediately installed in the plantation house. Never did she live in slave quarters nor was she ever treated as such.

Although Anna had lost her homeland, she found the new surroundings a pleasant substitute. She understood the system of planting, although it was on a much grander scale than that to which she had been accustomed. She also had a friend from Jolof, one of the two other women purchased by Kingsley, and who had traveled from Senegal with Anna. The two shared stories of their homeland in their own language, diminishing the pain of homesickness for both of them.

Anna also did not dwell on a lost childhood. She was carrying Kingsley's child by the time she arrived at the plantation. She was only one of many African women married to white plantation owners and she quickly adapted to her circumstances. She understood polygamous unions as that was also the practice in her culture. That her husband and other plantation owners had numerous concubines, co-wives, and children from those relationships, did not disturb her. She remained loyal to her husband and maintained a position of seniority at all times.

Although married to a white man, Anna's official status remained that of a slave until 1811 when she and her three children were officially emancipated. Kingsley worried that if he should be lost at sea, Anna and the children would be considered part of his estate and sold at auction. Anna already had the status of manager of the household and, as the years went by, she assumed more and more responsibility. As for her dignity, it had only been tarnished, not destroyed. As her managerial skills increased, she continued to gain respect from African Americans and whites alike. Her independent nature led to acquisition of her own land in Mandarin, a town across the river from Laurel Grove. Anna and her children—George, Martha, and Mary—lived in a comfortable two-story house. Once one herself, she now became an owner of twelve slaves housed on her compound. In addition to farming, she kept a poultry yard said to be "the greatest in the country."

Fortunately, Spanish laws gave Anna opportunities not found in the neighboring states of Georgia and the Carolinas. She was a free black woman entitled to specific rights and privileges. According to Schafer, she could hold property, manage plantations, testify and litigate in courts, and engage in business activities. She became a Catholic and formed extended kinship ties through godparent associations. She understood the system of networking with influential people as it was also a practice in her homeland.

In 1812, just as things were moving smoothly for Anna, groups of men known as Patriots were uniting in a revolutionary attempt to liberate Florida from Spain on behalf of the United States. The motivation not only was based on expansionist policies, but also was fueled by southern plantation owners angry about the liberal slave laws in Spanish Florida. Soldiers and sailors from the southern states crossed into Spanish North Florida taking the town of Fernandina and moving southward in hopes of conquering St. Augustine.

Soon after the uprising began, Zephaniah was seized and detained by the Patriots until he signed a pledge of support for the insurgents. When the paper was signed, Kingsley returned to his family and attempted to fortify Laurel Grove. Governor Sebastián Kindelán, however, decided to outsmart the rebels by ordering the Seminole Indians to attack surrounding settlements, an action he felt would drive the marauders away from battle to protect their own homelands. Although the tactic succeeded and the rebels withdrew, Laurel Grove was destroyed and more than forty Africans were taken as prisoners or killed by the Seminoles.

The following year danger again threatened Anna at her estate. If the rebels captured her and her children, they would be taken to Georgia and sold as slaves. This was unthinkable. Anna devised a plan which she shared with the captain of one of the Spanish gunboats sailing the St. Johns River. As soon as the rebels approached, Anna and her slaves emptied the house and hid the furniture in the woods. The children waited in seclusion with the slaves while Anna ran back and torched the house to prevent the enemy from using it as a stronghold. The plan worked and Anna and her family were safely transported to a fortification called San Nicolas across the river from Cowford (present-day Jacksonville). Anna was awarded a land grant for her heroic actions and within a few months Zephaniah, who had retreated from the danger, returned home.

In 1814, after a short stay in Fernandina, the Kingsley family was taken by ship to their new plantation on the northern tip of Fort George Island. The plantation had been evacuated by the rebel leader John H. McIntosh and, though in disrepair, presented a magnificent appearance to the homeless family.

This was to be the home Anna and the children would come to know and love. In 1824 a fourth blessed event came to Anna and Zephaniah in the form of a baby boy they named John Maxwell. Anna was thirty-one at the time and her youngest daughter, Mary, was thirteen. The plantation did well under Kingsley management, expanding to include comfortable tabby-constructed houses for the slave families. A separate building with a connecting walkway to the main plantation house was built for Anna and the children. The house, known as "Ma'am Anna House," was also the main cooking area for the plantation house. This was an acceptable arrangement for Anna. Her superior status was retained, yet the arrangement provided Zephaniah an opportunity to move freely with his co-wives. Additionally, members of Zephaniah's white family were now becoming involved with plantation work. His sister Isabel's sons, George B. and Zephaniah C. Gibbs, were regular visitors as was Charles J. McNeill, the son of Zephaniah's sister Martha. The nephews were interested in plantation management and worked closely with Zephaniah on business matters as well as practical aspects involving farming.

The fact that all family members recognized and accepted the extended family situation on some level was exhibited at the baptism of John Maxwell when he was five years of age. His godmother was his sister Mary, his godfather his uncle Zephaniah C. Gibbs. John Maxwell's niece was baptized at the same ceremony. The niece, young Mary Martha Mattier, was the daughter of Fatimah McGundo Kingsley. Fatimah was conceived by Zephaniah and one of his co-wives, Munsilna McGundo, making Fatimah a half-sister to Anna's children, and her child, Mary Martha, John Maxwell's niece.[3]

By the time of John Maxwell's birth in 1824, Florida was in its third year as a territory of the United States. With the departure of the Spanish, race relations changed under the new government. In 1823 Zephaniah was appointed to the Territorial Council where his concern about race relations grew to enormous alarm. Gone were the liberal race laws of the Spanish regime. The new government considered all blacks to be slaves. There was no room for "free" people of color. The laws prohibited interracial marriages excluding children resulting from such unions from any inheritance. Another law punished white men found guilty of having sexual encounters with black women.

When an 1829 law restricted emancipation, Kingsley was distraught. He believed in and practiced manumission and Anna and his children deserved to remain free as he intended. To protect his family he deeded Fort George Island to his son George in 1831 and divided other properties to his daughters and members of his extended family. During this time he discovered a program in Haiti that was recruiting free blacks to help restore the island's prosperity. Calling the family together, plans were made. To further ensure property rights, Kingsley took back Fort George Island from his son and sold it to his nephew, Kingsley B. Gibbs. A residence was established for Gibbs' brother Zephaniah with supervision of eighty-nine slaves given to nephew Charles J. McNeill.

Zephaniah made frequent trips to Haiti purchasing tracks of land for cultivation. In 1836 his son George and George's wife, Anatoile, joined him there. In 1837 Anna and John Maxwell, as well as several co-wives and extended family members, departed for Haiti. Mary and Martha, both married to white men of Scottish descent, remained in Florida to begin new lives of their own.

The move from Fort George Island carried its own pain for Anna, different from the physical and emotional trauma of being stolen from her homeland but equally difficult. She had lived at Fort George Island for almost twenty-five years. Her three older children had grown up there and George had, for a time, maintained ownership. Her youngest

Anna Kingsley's house on Fort George Island was linked to the principal building by a covered walkway. (Photo by Karen Harvey)

child was born at the plantation. John Maxwell was thirteen, the same age as Anna when she was abducted from her homeland, as they sailed to a new land unknown to everyone except Zephaniah.

A plantation called Mayorasgo de Koka was established to produce products including sugar, cotton, citrus, and corn. Anna lived in the settlement of Cabaret Creek. Her now legendary beach house was a place where she spent quiet days lounging in African-style long gowns and gold jewelry. She lived in well-deserved comforts supported by profits from Mayorasgo de Koka and income from the Florida plantations.

Zephaniah Kingsley died on September 13, 1842, at age seventy-eight. He and Anna had been married for thirty-seven years and she was now fifty years old. As Zephaniah predicted before his death, there was great disagreement from his white relatives over the distribution of his estate, estimated in the millions of dollars, much of which was designated for the mulatto families living in Haiti. The case went to the Florida Supreme Court which upheld Kingsley's will. Disputes continued, however, and in 1846 George Kingsley sailed for Jacksonville to mediate the situation. Unfortunately, the ship was caught in a severe storm and George, age thirty-nine, was drowned.

Shortly after George's death Anna returned to Florida and purchased a twenty-two-acre farm, Chesterfield, on the east bank of the St. Johns River. She was near her daughters, each of whom lived successfully on well-run plantations, and close to extended family members living along the river.

Although Anna was undoubtedly the matriarch of the family, law required she work through a white guardian. Her guardian was her son-in-law John Sammis, Mary's husband. However, Anna was, as expected, in charge of the large clan.

In 1860 Anna sold Chesterfield and moved to Point St. Isabel, her daughter Martha's plantation just a short distance north along the river. Martha was ill and needed care. Anna was sixty-seven and herself in poor health. She was content with her life, however, living in her own quarters on Martha's plantation and raising her granddaughter, Isabella, John Maxwell's child. He remained in Haiti caring for Mayorasgo de Koka. The unique settlement along the shores of the St. Johns River reminded her so much of her homeland Senegal. Stretching for three miles between the plantations of her two daughters, the community included numerous households of free blacks as well as members of the Kingsley family. Many were former slaves from the Fort George Island plantation. All had formed patron-client bonds reminiscent of the lifestyle Anna remembered from her childhood.

The Civil War took its toll on the Kingsley family and all free blacks in northeastern Florida. As a strong Union supporter, Anna was in danger from Confederate forces. She, her daughters, and their families were eventually forced to leave their homes in Florida to seek safety in Philadelphia and New York.

Returning to Florida at the end of the war in 1865, the family found major destruction and legal difficulties in reclaiming their property. Forever diligent, however, Anna and her family worked to restore their lives and regain prosperity. In February 1870 Anna's daughter Martha died and Anna followed her in July. With all her hardships, she had lived her life well and left a great legacy to all her descendants. One grandson, Egbert Sammis, was elected to the Florida State Senate in 1884. Others continued the legacy of productive farming and conscientious care of employees who by then all fell in the category of free blacks.

Although Anna's first—and probably only—sight of St. Augustine occurred in 1806 when Kingsley's ship docked to register her in Spanish Florida, her close proximity and contacts with the Florida capital kept her aware of the little Spanish town. Indeed, the Kingsley name spread to the town through Kingsley Beatty Gibbs, Zephaniah's nephew. Known as "King," the young Gibbs arrived with his family as Florida was becoming a territory of the United States. His father, George Gibbs, was appointed Customs House collector within a week of the change of flags from Spain to the United States in July 1821. King was only seventeen when he became deputy clerk of the Superior Court under his father. He was twenty-two years of age when he served on a committee appointing Judge Joseph Lee Smith as a federal judge.

In 1839, as Zephaniah Kingsley's family relocated to Haiti, King purchased the Fort George Island plantation. When Zephaniah died in 1843, he left his nephew one-twelfth of the final distribution of the bulk of his estate. During that year King won a seat in the Florida Territorial Legislature and over the next few years continued to work in and around the community of St. Augustine and in northeast Florida.

Anna Madgigine Jai Kingsley, nee Anta Majigeen Njaay, became an inspiration for African Americans in Northeast Florida. Her determination and independent spirit reaped the fruits of the harvest. Her love of freedom and family kept the Kingsley clan strong and fortunate. Anna never looked back, instead she always saw the bounty that lay ahead of her.

Kingsley Plantation, where Anna spent almost twenty-five happy years of her life, is now owned by the National Park Service and can be seen on Fort George Island on the northeast coast of Florida. Her memory lives on.

A FAMILY VERSION OF ANNA KINGSLEY'S STORY

Anna's story as written here is a plausible version of her removal from Senegal and subsequent delivery into slavery. However, it raises many questions including the ease with which she was abducted and the immediacy of her selection as the bride of Zephaniah Kingsley.

How could Anna have been stolen from the safe environment of her father's village without some warning? Anna was the daughter of a man of status—albeit the ruler of a shrinking kingdom. How could the warring tribes gotten close enough to "steal" Anna? Zephaniah Kingsley was indeed a slave trader, but how did he happen to find and choose Anna to be his bride?

In Schafer's revised and expanded edition of the Anna Kingsley story he identifies Jolof as the homeland for Anna explaining not all historians agree on the exact location in Africa. Schafer chose the ship *Sally* as the vessel transporting Anna to Cuba since it was documented as a ship containing an unusually large number of African females. In pointing out the questionable theories he acknowledges other scenarios. However, this is the family side of the story as told by George W. Gibbs IV, a direct descendant of Kingsley Beatty Gibbs, Zephaniah's nephew who acquired the Fort George plantation in 1839.

Zephaniah Kingsley was a slave trader who had developed relationships with African tribesmen who were in the business of selling slaves. This was frequently the case in that time period. White slave traders dealt with African men who captured and sold other Africans probably from warring tribes. It is Gibbs' belief that Zephaniah dealt directly with Anna's father for the procurement of human cargo.

It was rare for the dealers themselves to travel on the slave ships, but Gibbs believes Zephaniah did exactly that and negotiated with the king for Anna and the unusually large number of women that were taken from the village along with Anna. If this is true, Anna's father ensured the safety of Anna by promising her to Zephaniah as his wife. If so, it would also explain how Anna was selected by Zephaniah so expediently and why she was treated with deference immediately upon arrival in Florida. It also would preclude the possibility of Anna seeing her father killed.

Gibbs summarizes the situation candidly, "I find it difficult to believe that Zephaniah would have spotted this girl who had just been released from the hold of a slave ship after suffering the horror and humiliation and unsanitary conditions associated with the transportation of humans. After months at sea with only saltwater baths, standing in the heat on the streets of Havana, and said he 'there is my bride standing over there.' That is ridiculous. And how would he know of her royal status? Who would have told him this and why would he believe who ever told him this wild tale?"

Gibbs continues by noting, "The history of their lives in Florida is much easier to authenticate and (it) is undisputed that Anna was of royal descent. She was treated by the whites and blacks as royalty. This did not happen because Zephaniah was told a wild tale by his young bride. The Africans who would have known the true story first hand."

Some discrepancies between family lore and fact may never be known. Anna herself stated in 1835 she was born in Senegal. How she was captured or chosen to be Zephaniah Kingsley's wife may never be known. She was indeed the daughter of a man of high status. Bennett wrote that Anna Jai's father was referred to as a "chief of Madagascar," who was also rumored to have helped Kingsley procure slaves.

As for her description as a tall, jet black beautiful woman, almost anyone who writes about Anna Jai Kingsley describes her in a similar manner. Folklore aside, a description of her can be found in Child's *Letters From New York* indicating she was indeed a striking woman by anyone's standards. Also, by anyone's standards Anna proved to be an excellent mother, effective plantation manager, and thoughtful business woman.

❧

ABBIE M. BROOKS
Waif or Willful Woman? (late 1800s–1914)

In a document dating back to the 1870s Abbie Brooks described herself as "a waif floating about upon the shores of a fathomless sea." Earlier when she was thirty-five, an 1865 diary entry revealed she made a mistake which "she could not remove with tears of blood. . . ."

That mistake plagued Abbie her entire life and blanketed the masterful writer, indefatigable researcher, and uninhibited traveler with a shroud of mystery.

When Abbie Brooks died in St. Augustine in 1914, no one knew the details of her birth or background. In fact it was not until the end of the century that curiosity led to new discoveries about the secretive person who was the first American woman to research Florida's history in the archives of Seville and Madrid, Spain. It was known she frequented St. Augustine from 1830 until her death. She had authored *Petals Plucked from Sunny Climes* and other freelance material about St. Augustine and Florida, published in newspapers throughout the south and the east coast of the United States. There was, however, little known about Abbie Brooks also identified as Silvia Sunshine.

In life Abbie M. Brooks was consumed by a quest for anonymity. A century after her death her identity was revealed and facts about the shrouded life of the writer, researcher, and traveler surfaced.

We now know Abbie was born July 11, 1830, in Cooperstown, Pennsylvania. Her birth name was Abigail Mary Lindley. Thanks to a decade of persistent research by Yvonne and Richard Punnett as reported in the *East Florida Gazette*, February 1999, we meet Abbie's family and we know the deep, dark secret that ostracized Abigail Lindley from those closest to her.

The secret: Abbie was the mother of an illegitimate child.

The disgrace this "unspeakable" deed brought to an otherwise principled and socially admirable family drove Abbie from her home and kept her private life hidden even as she went out into the world as a great adventurer. The child, named Hortense and called Ortie, was conceived in 1855 when Abbie was twenty-five. At one point she wrote in her diary, "My kindred have handed me to God for mercy and shown none themselves."[1]

Despite her family problems—or because of them—Abbie opened doors that might otherwise have been closed to her. She traveled throughout Florida in the late 1870s and wrote of her visits in *Petals* as if she was whisked along superhighways speeding her from location to location. Although her travels took place over a series of years, she writes as if they were one continuous itinerary. Even as she delightfully describes the 1870s locales, she is mesmerized by the history preceding her visits. One wonders if she used spacecrafts transcending time. It takes only three pages to leave Atlanta, Georgia, and land in Fernandina, Florida, during which flight we learn about General Oglethorpe's stay in Savannah in 1733 (seven years before his attack on St. Augustine's Castillo de San Marcos). Then we're told of the visit by naturalist John Bartram to St. Simon's Island in 1744 just before we are whisked to Fernandina where Revolutionary War hero Nathanael Greene spent his last days. None of her daring swoops and dives into history detract from her 1870s travels. Her descriptions are word paintings, her destinations interesting. Observing the departure of the Indians who, for three years, had been incarcerated in the old Spanish fort, then called Fort Marion, she imagines both the past and future of the stone structure. "As in time past, the old fort, that has lifted its turrets unmoved for centuries to the fierce gales which visit the coast, will again become the home of the lizard, a resort for bats, the abode of the owl, whose shrill screechings and weird movements make the darkness of night more suggestive of a ghoul-haunted castle, where unhappy spirits are supposed to assemble when 'coarser spirits wrapped in clay' are snoring to the ascending and descending scale of unwritten sounds."[2]

She writes as if she were platting a trip for the reader, although she obviously visited many different places at many different times. Her travels take her from Jacksonville and the St. Johns River to "that peculiar stream, the Oklawaha," on to Silver Springs before it was a resort, down to the Everglades, and over to the Gulf Coast. She visits Tampa and Pensacola touching more of Florida than most natives could in a lifetime.

Petals Plucked from Sunny Climes was published in 1880 under the playful pseudonym Silvia Sunshine. It was printed twice, then more or less shelved to gather dust. Interest in Abbie lay smoldering until *Petals* was raised from the ashes in 1976 when the book was chosen as one of twenty-five rare and out-of-print books to be republished as a facsimile edition in 1976 by the Florida Bicentennial Commission. Even then, little was known about her as evidenced in the preface by Dr. Samuel Procter who wrote, "So complete is the mystery of her background that Richard A. Martin, who has written the introduction to this facsimile edition, after much diligent research was unable to find almost nothing at all about Abbie M. Brooks." At that time Procter and Martin both bemoan the fact that little is known of her education, professional career, or personal life. Martin cites the date she moved to St. Augustine (late 1890s) and gives an address where she was presumed to live in the town, but found little more than that basic information.

What they did know, in addition to her Florida travels, was that she also visited Cuba in 1875 and she loved Florida's history enough to educate herself in the Spanish language. In 1891, at age sixty, Abbie sailed to Spain, remaining for a year as she diligently copied records from the Archives of the Indies in Seville covering the periods of discovery and colonization of Florida from 1500 to 1810. Although preceded by Buckingham Smith (1810–1871), St. Augustine humanitarian, diplomat, and scholar who researched Florida-related documents in the Spanish archives of Mexico and Madrid, Spain, Abbie was the first American woman to collect such invaluable information.

Aided by translator Mrs. Annie Averette, the result was five volumes of transcriptions sold in 1901 to the Library of Congress for three hundred dollars. From those volumes Abbie extracted materials for the publication of *The Unwritten History of Old St. Augustine*, printed in 1907 by The Record Company of St. Augustine. An unfortunate aside to that accomplishment was that the Library of Congress destroyed the manuscripts in 1983. Their explanation—they had received copies of the original Spanish documents which made Abbie's redundant.[3] In fact, scholars have rarely used her research since she did not always cite the source material. That does not, however, diminish her courageous efforts and contributions.

It is through the recent research of Yvonne and Richard Punnett that Abbie gained a life of her own so long after her mortal death. Numerous facts were brought to light. For example, Abbie's father, Alanson Lindley, had three daughters, Abigail, Helen, and Lucretta (Lucy). They found that Alanson was an educator, which perhaps accounted for some of Abbie's thirst for literature. She was well educated, voraciously read history, poetry, and novels current at the time such as those by Charles Dickens and William Thackery. She also played the piano, spoke French fluently, and taught herself Spanish.[4]

Her father was a strict Presbyterian, a practice she faithfully followed. In St. Augustine she was a member of Memorial Presbyterian Church during her twilight years. Her spiritual beliefs surface frequently in her writing. Excerpts from a diary in the St. Augustine Historical Society described by Jean Parker Waterbury in the *East Florida Gazette* reveal much about Abbie's religious convictions. While in Spain in 1904 (at age seventy-five), Abbie made an entry on "the Holy Sabbath a day

Abbie Brooks lived a life of mystery. This is the only known photograph of her. (Photo from St. Augustine Historical Society)

of rest, when the women are coming from market. Everything moves as though there was no God to love or obey."

Later that year she prepared to embark on her voyage back to the United States. She wrote, "May God protect me and bring me in safety to my own country."

In her 1870 diary when she was alone in Nashville, Tennessee, with no family and no money she wrote, "What service have I rendered to my God? Who has benefitted by my presence?"[5]

Most startling in her personal relationship with God are the following comments written while in St. Augustine in 1905: "A woman is a powerful influence for good or evil."; "Never be a vulture feeding on the decaying carcass."; "Obey means maternity. Obey your husband in the worship of the Lord."

Waterbury notes these are probably sentences remembered from sermons or books. Whatever the origin, they are strong statements coming from a woman who has lived a full life alone guided by her own interests and ambitions.[6]

In the obituary of Abbie's father it was noted that Alanson was "a man who despised shams and hypocrisy in all their forms. Honest, straightforward and truthful in all his dealings in the world and in the church, he had little or no charity for inconsistency in others."[7]

That certainly gives insight into Abbie's need to distance herself from the family. Research also suggests Abbie took refuge with her aunt Phoebe Spencer, mentioned briefly in her diary, leading one to believe that exile was not total, although nearly so.

And what of Abbie's daughter? After years of search, the Punnetts believed they had concluded their quest when they found the child. Abbie's daughter, Ortie Lewis, was mentioned in sister Lucy's will as the recipient of the residue of her estate. At that time, Ortie was listed as living in Geneva, Ohio. A trip to Geneva resulted in the discovery that Ortie had been adopted by David A. Bacon and his wife Laura. Of all the sixteen children the couple adopted, Ortie was the only one mentioned by name in Bacon's will. It said, "Besides providing for his own large family, he made his home an asylum for some sixteen other children that were in need of such a place; one of whom is Mrs. Lewis (Ortie) of Geneva, who ever clung to him even down to death, with all the undying affection of a daughter."[8]

But the story of Ortie hardly ends there. Discoveries in 2001 show Ortie was actually born in Fort Ann, New York, while Abbie was living with her aunt Phoebe. Yvonne Punnett believes Abbie and the baby left New York after two years, traveling to Ohio with two of Phoebe's siblings. It was in Geneva, Ohio, that the baby, possibly with a different given name, was adopted by the Bacon family and raised as Hortence "Ortie" Bacon. Ortie married a man with the surname of Lewis. Their first child was given the middle name of Lindley indicating Ortie knew something of her birth mother's background.[9]

The mystery shrouding Abbie Brooks all those years has in many ways overshadowed the full significance of her contributions. *Petals Plucked from Sunny Climes* presents intriguing and picturesque glimpses into the look and life of 1870s Florida. *The Unwritten History of Old St. Augustine* is proof of her fortitude in pursuing Florida history through the Spanish archives. The fact that her research is considered "insignificant" today does not diminish the work she accomplished.

There is much, though, to consider about Abigail Mary Lindley Brooks. Was she wronged by banishment for the "crime" of unwed motherhood? Did she perhaps simply choose to follow her dreams and take the road less traveled? If indeed Abbie gave Ortie up for adoption when the child was two or three years old, she had plenty of time to make a decision to do so. Whether it was a solitary decision or one forced by her family values, Abbie's choice was to go forth and experience life without the responsibility of a child.

Yvonne Punnett believes that Abbie would never have accomplished what she did if she had kept the child. But Abbie also didn't want to experience life entirely on her own. In later years Abbie wanted to marry. Punnett said, "She desperately wanted a companion." Referring to an unrequited love affair in 1870 with a wandering salesman, Punnett wrote, "Abbie thought she had one."

That relationship is the only one Abbie mentioned in her diaries and its failure left her without a companion. But it hardly left her distraught. The ambitious Miss Brooks left her teaching job to enter a world denied to women of that day. She sought a position at a book-selling firm to pursue a career in the canvassing trade, a field akin to current literary agencies. She said, "I fear I have chosen a stormy path. . . ." But that did not stop her ambitious tenacity and once again demonstrated her pioneering spirit.

Should we remember her as a valiant trooper or the victim of narrowminded callousness? She fought the battle of total ostracization akin to shunning in the closed society of the Amish. But at no time in her writing does she complain or sound bitter. She evidently made her own choices, particularly in light of the new evidence that she kept her child for two or three years. She courageously accepted her fate and moved on with her life.

Do we feel sorry for her? No, we simply applaud her works based on her worldwide adventures.

The Punnetts' research also uncovered numerous descendants of Ortie Lewis, none of whom knew of Abbie prior to being contacted by the Punnetts. Included among the six visiting St. Augustine in November 2000 were great-grandchildren and great-great-grandchildren of Abbie Brooks. All paid their respects to the ancestor they never knew at the small graveside gathering.

At the newly dedicated headstone at her burial place in Evergreen Cemetery in St. Augustine, Owene Weber, a historian compiling a biography of Abbie Brooks, quoted one of Abbie's diary entries as stating, "I have entirely abandoned the idea of ever doing anything by which my name may be perpetuated."

For once, Abbie Brooks was wrong. Her name has and will be perpetuated despite the obstacles she encountered along the way.

THE REST OF THE STORY

Abbie Brooks seems to have chosen more than one way to perpetuate her name. She died at 50 Water Street, the home of Isabella and Charles Hopkins. Hopkins, the founder of The Record Company, publishers of Brooks' *Unwritten History*, was also a deacon of Memorial Presbyterian Church, the church Abbie attended during the latter years of her life. As she reached her final years, her infirmities required extensive care. Hopkins first arranged for food to be delivered to her in her own dwelling, then welcomed her into his home where she spent the last years of her life under the care of Isabella.

Leonora Stoddard, the granddaughter of Isabella and Charles Hopkins, remembers stories about Abbie who her grandparents described as a very mysterious woman. Now, years after Abbie's death, visitors to the house report feeling a presence in the room where Abbie spent her last days. Some actually have seen the presence of an elderly lady in a white dress believed to be the mysterious Miss Brooks.

Did Abbie decide to perpetuate her spirit as well as her name? That is a mystery still left to be solved.

CHAPTER IV
Stirring Spanish Waters

❧

MARIA DOMINGA DE ZÉSPEDES
The Governor's Daughter Who Dared (1784–1787)

Maria Dominga de Zéspedes, the Spanish teenager with "languishing eyes," lived a dream that turned into her father's worst nightmare. The lovely young daughter of the new governor of East Florida saw the trip from Havana, Cuba, to the New World as an adventure equal to that of a damsel in distress swept up from danger by a brave knight.

Dominga, her sister Maria Josepha, and brothers Vizente and Antonio, set sail for East Florida with their mother Doña Maria Concepción and father Vizente Manuel de Zéspedes, the newly appointed governor of East Florida. The brothers were young officers in the Spanish military who were delighted to accompany their father on an important mission. The sisters were of marriageable age and companions for their mother.

The time was 1784 and Florida had been returned to Spain after two decades of British rule. It was a difficult transition for the Spanish since the colonies north of the peninsula had won their freedom from Great Britain and were now the independent country of the United States of America. Spain's hold on Florida was tenuous at best and Governor Zéspedes faced many challenges. How much of a challenge he faced with his own daughter Dominga was yet to be determined as the family arrived in Florida and the governor began his term of office.

With the mix of young men in St. Augustine consisting of departing British soldiers and incoming Spanish troops, Dominga was well aware of the strict codes of behavior limiting social and political freedom of young women. She was heavily guarded to protect her innocence and her reputation. But, despite the power and protective nature of her father, Dominga proved to be a passionate young woman who not only disregarded social mores but defied her family and the Catholic church.

An account of life in Zéspedes's St. Augustine home is offered in a personal letter written by General Nathanael Greene, a renowned officer in America's War of Independence. Greene was visiting Florida during a trip to investigate property violations of his land on Cumberland Island, Georgia. He and his companion, Colonel Benjamin Hawkins, were American dignitaries and it was the duty of Governor Zéspedes to treat them accordingly. At a gubernatorial dinner hosted by Doña Concepción and daughters Dominga and Josepha, both Greene and Hawkins were overly impressed. In her book *Zéspedz in East Florida, 1784–1790*, Helen Hornbeck Tanner quotes the contents of Greene's letter describing his visit.

> *We were introduced to his Lady and daughters and compliments flew from side to side like a shuttle cock in the hands of good players. You know I am not very excellent at fine speeches. My stock was soon exhausted; but what I lacked in conversation I made up in bowing.*
>
> *The Governnante (Governor's wife) is about fifty-five, as cheerful as a Girl of sixteen, and enters with spirit and pleasure into all the amusements of the young people. She is sister to the Vice Roy of Mexico and highly respected both from her family and pleasing manners. The daughters are not handsome, their complexion is rather tawny but they have got sweet languishing Eyes. They look as if they could love with great violence. They sang and played on the Harpsichord and did every thing to please if not to inspire softer emotions. Hawkins professed himself smitten.*[1]

The languishing eyes of Dominga apparently did reveal she could love with "great violence" as she later proved. Although Dominga and Josepha received much attention from the hundreds of soldiers in St. Augustine, the two girls were carefully chaperoned in public and attended social functions only in the presence of their parents. Despite watchful eyes, Dominga's heart was captured by an Irish solder of the Hibernian garrison stationed in St. Augustine. The object of the shared affection was Juan O'Donovan.

As early as February 1785, O'Donovan had approached the governor suggesting marriage to Dominga. The governor delivered a fatherly speech about meeting the demands of status and supporting his daughter in the manner to which she had become accustomed. To the governor he had delayed the inevitable until he could eliminate the presence of the young suitor. To O'Donovan it was a refusal of his request for marriage. The formal meeting ended with nothing resolved.

It was in the spring when the governor further learned of his daughter's passion for the young Irish soldier. The whispers started in the garrison officers' quarters and spread via the small town grapevine to Dominga's brothers Vizente and Antonio. O'Donovan made the mistake of boasting about his plans to elope with Dominga if her father refused his request to marry her.

At about the same time, O'Donovan alerted the governor of his request to resign his position in St. Augustine in order to return to Ireland. The suspicious father regarded the request as a threat or possibly a diversionary tactic. Whatever the intent, Zéspedes did not want the bold young soldier taking his daughter away from him so he made arrangements for him to be transferred from St. Augustine as quickly as possible.

It was during a formal dinner celebration on May 29 when Dominga and O'Donovan deviously managed to marry—in the first of three ceremonies. When Zéspedes realized that Dominga was missing from the party he sent his son to find her. Vizente located his sister and her lover at the home of Chief Engineer Mariano LaRoque who was absent from town that evening. His wife, Doña Angela Huet, a close friend of the Zéspedes family, was sympathetic to

It is in this house that Dominga de Zéspedes lived while her father was governor. Business transacted here by the governor included the murder investigation involving Catalina Morain. (Copy of sketch from author's collection)

Dominga's emotional predicament.

The two women and O'Donovan devised a plot to formally unite the lovers in matrimony and legitimize it in the eyes of the Catholic church. A servant woman was sent to get the local priest, Father O'Reilly, on the pretext that Doña Angela had been injured in an accident. Upon arriving at the house the priest walked into the inner room where Dominga and O'Donovan stood with clasped hands reciting marriage vows. The secret ceremony became legitimate as planned when it was verified that vows were stated in the presence of a priest and other witnesses. All present agreed that was the case.

Vizente returned to the festivities and relayed the details of the event to his parents. Doña Concepción immediately was overcome with emotion and tearfully left the party with Josepha by her side comforting her. O'Donovan did not receive any understanding from the injured and irate parents. Instead he was arrested for breaking the law by marrying without the consent of a superior officer. Dominga was returned to her home crying emotionally. Innocent Father O'Reilly was distraught at being a part of such a conspiracy even though it had been unintentional on his part.

Dominga was deeply loved by her father who was torn between his compassion for his daughter and his rigid adherence to Spanish customs and laws. His daughter's decision to wed an unworthy "foreigner" further complicated the situation. The event left the powerful governor woefully powerless.

Tanner claims Zéspedes was concerned about the local town gossip that would circulate the next day. She wrote:

> His daughter's honor now assumed more importance than his own pride, and he concluded that above all he wanted assurance that she was really properly married. Later that night, he took Father O'Reilly to the home of Father Hasset and asked to have a second marriage performed immediately. Father Hasset an ecclesiastical judge had doubts about this procedure but acceded to the governor's vehement demands and promised to report the whole affair to the king, assuming full responsibility if this was an improper course of action. Then Governor Zéspedes returned home to pace up and down while Father O'Reilly escorted O'Donovan from his quarters. After a second marriage ceremony had been performed under the supervision of Father Hasset, the bride and groom returned to their separate imprisonment. Zéspedes vowed he'd retain custody of his daughter until he learned the king's order concerning this unprecedented marriage.[2]

Following normal military procedure, O'Donovan was exiled to Havana while the governor awaited the decision from King Charles III. O'Donovan was an Irishman serving the Spanish Crown as a paid soldier with the Hibernian Regiment. His standing could hardly compare to that of his new father-in-law. O'Donovan was, however, a reality with which the authorities were forced to contend. Contending with the wishes of Dominga was another matter entirely for Zéspedes.

It is unclear why Zéspedes changed his attitude toward his new son-in-law, but he sent communications to Havana asking for the charges to be absolved against O'Donovan. Perhaps his daughter's heartbreak was more than he could endure. Or perhaps he realized that the second marriage had made the first even more binding.

In June of 1786 the decision was rendered to release O'Donovan and return him to the Hibernian Regiment. It was not until November that news of his freedom reached St. Augustine. Unfortunately fate was still frowning on the two young lovers. The ship carrying O'Donovan to his waiting bride was forced by storms to turn back to Cuba. By the time O'Donovan successfully reached St. Augustine's shores, two years had elapsed since the night of the clandestine ceremony.

Zéspedes had no recourse but to accept the situation and chose to ease the situation by making his daughter as comfortable as possible and gave her a wedding gift of a new house on the bayfront. Dominga's mother took charge of decorating and furnishing the home and a gardener was engaged to prepare the outside to make it more appealing.

Dominga apparently was still not satisfied with the situation and asked that the nuptials be repeated a third time with a church mass. The Catholic Church at the time had strict guidelines on when such services could be performed. Dominga's request was not granted initially as permission from the king was required. Once royal permission was granted Dominga was clearly pregnant. In November of 1787 a third marriage ceremony was performed by Father Hasset. On February 9, 1788, Dominga gave birth to a son. He was proudly baptized Juan Vizente Maria Bernardo Domingo Begnigno O'Donovan.

Dominga's story provides insights into the limited power a young woman of noble birth could expect in the 1700s. However, Dominga demonstrated that power of persistence and passion can match even the greatest patriarchal power system.

🦢

CATALINA MORAIN
Seamstress or Seductress? (1785–1790)

The wind was blowing through the dark and narrow passageways of St. Augustine's streets on a cold autumn night in 1785. A man hurried from the stone fort clutching his dark cloak around his shoulders. He turned onto the street called San Carlos heading toward the lane of the treasurer when men in hooded capes threw him to the ground and viciously attacked him with knives.

With the deed accomplished, the villains fled leaving the body crumpled on the ground. But Lieutenant Delaney was not dead. Barely conscious he heard the footsteps retreating and waited until only the sound of wind rustling the November leaves prevailed on the street.

Lieutenant Guillermo Delaney was an Irish soldier in the Hibernian Regiment. He was on his way to the home of a woman who had charmed him. Her name was Catalina Morain and it was to her house that he crawled after the attack. He reached the dwelling and collapsed at the door. It was there Catalina found him near death.[1]

The ensuing investigation proved to be disastrous for the British-born young woman who earned her living as a seamstress in Spanish St. Augustine. It also proved to be an albatross around the neck of Governor Vizente Manual de Zéspedes who had arrived in St. Augustine in June 1784.

Florida was returned to Spain after twenty years of British rule. Zéspedes arrived to take control as the British residents departed and new Spaniards arrived. The little St. Augustine settlement, already more than two hundred years old, was a garrison town filled with troops and Catalina Morain was a single Anglo-American woman attracting the attentions of the soldiers. She lived in a rented room in a large home on the bayfront and since her business involved sewing the uniforms for the soldiers, it was not unusual to see the men of the town coming and going from her residence.

Finding the brutally stabbed soldier at her door posed numerous problems for everyone. Catalina was shocked by the attempted murder. Zéspedes, occupied with governmental duties and family concerns, did not welcome the additional disruption of his time. Neighbors and soldiers were called in for questioning. The town was abuzz with gossip.

Delaney was interviewed immediately as the most important witness. Considering the darkness and the abruptness of the attack, he was only able to report that his assailants wore the standard clothing of the military. In a town of 2,700 with half the population military, that was of little help. Delaney suggested it might have been a case of mistaken identity, but local officials thought otherwise. Someone wanted Delaney dead. Or if it was a mistake, who was the intended victim?

Investigations of the townspeople and other soldiers involved failed to determine specific clues. When Catalina was questioned about the incident she implicated two soldiers: Pablo de Martos and Ramon Cucarella. Considering the lack of concrete evidence otherwise, the two men were immediately imprisoned while the inquiry continued. They were later released, however, as both had verifiable alibis.

Further investigation of the situation indicated the possible guilt of two soldiers who showed interest in the affections of Catalina. One of the two already had posed problems for Zéspedes.

He was Distinguished Sergeant Juan Sivelly who publically defied the standards set by the governor. Six months before the Delaney attack Sivelly had been warned against keeping company with a servant girl. Defiantly he rode past the governor's house with Isabel Shivers, an attractive employee in the home of Governor Patrick Tonyn, the last British governor of East Florida. Zéspedes was outraged at the flagrant disobedience of the young soldier. Sivelly was not only cavorting with a British servant girl, but he was out of uniform and riding beyond the city boundaries.

The obvious misbehavior was exacerbated by the fact that Isabel was Protestant and of a lower class than Sivelly who was of noble birth. Zéspedes had no choice but to take the young man out of harms way and put him under temporary arrest. It was six months after release from the charges of misconduct that he was again in serious trouble due to the Delaney attack.

The second man incriminated was Corporal Francisco Moraga. His story further complicated the mystery. His name was brought to the attention of Zéspedes and the officials because the testimony of witnesses indicated the infatuation of both Sivelly and Moraga toward Catalina. In fact, it seems both of them had a motive of simple jealousy as a reason to want the other dead. Thus either one of them could have committed the crime believing they were eliminating the undesired suitor and attacking Delaney by mistake.

Adding to the confusion was a play production in rehearsal in nearby St. Francis Barracks on Marine Street the night of the attack. Moraga was seen by witnesses at play rehearsal. But rather than an alibi it became a source of suspicion since he passed by the house where

Catalina lived on the return path to his quarters. Moraga also came under suspicion because he said he had not been to see Catalina the night of the attack. The owners of the home in which Catalina rented a room refuted the statement arguing that Moraga not only was in the house but was armed at the time. The wife of the home owner, Señora Gomila, recalled Moraga used his cutlass to sharpen a quill for her. The guards at the fort were unable to substantiate Moraga's story because they had been sleeping at the approximate time of attack.

As allegations mounted against the two soldiers, word leaked out that Catalina was known to have many admirers and suddenly the focus on Sivelly and Moraga faded. Was Catalina involved in the attack? Did she perhaps encourage the assault? As the days moved on, Catalina became the target of suspicion. It made no difference that she was at home and it was to her door the injured man had crawled.

Lieutenant Delaney died of his wounds shortly after New Years 1786 and Zéspedes found himself in the midst of a murder trial. He was in a legal dilemma from which he could not extricate himself. His pleas for legal assistance went unanswered and he was left afloat at sea in his own little lifeboat. With no way to prove or disprove the innocence or guilt of any of the suspects, he chose to imprison both Moraga and Catalina. Sivelly was slipping easily out of the ropes of justice. He had been released from prison after Governor Tonyn and his household, including Isabel, departed East Florida. Despite his antics Zéspedes had approved Sivelly for promotion to lieutenant, a promotion anticipated due to his higher status of nobility. For Zéspedes the promotion freed him to reassign Sivelly out of East Florida and out of his jurisdiction.

As for Catalina it didn't matter that she was the one to whom the hapless Delaney crawled. Her life was forever changed whether guilty of wrongdoing or not. She was thrown in jail for no other reason than twisting the truth by implicating Martos and Cucarella, both of whom had alibis. That made her crime one of perjury.

Moraga may or may not have committed a crime, but he was left to suffer for whomever did. Both Corporal Moraga and Catalina Morain remained in jail until the departure of Governor Zéspedes in June 1790—four and a half years after the attack on Delaney.

Catalina was a seamstress and she may have been a seductress, but she certainly was not a murderer. The scales of justice were badly tipped against her. ❧

The story of Catalina Morain has been told and debated by tale-tellers and actors in and around St. Augustine. In recent years a new twist was added to the murder mystery. A deathbed confession by a soldier involved in the incident ostensibly clears Moraga's name and lends credence to Catalina's innocence of complicity in the crime.[2]

Although the name of the individual is not known, the discovery of the document is further indication that Moraga was innocent and nothing justified Catalina's years of imprisonment.

CHAPTER V

Enterprising Women

❧

XIMÉNEZ-FATIO HOUSE
The Women Within (1780s–Present)

A stately two-story structure overlooking a narrow brick road named Aviles Street bears the hyphenated name Ximénez-Fatio. In addition to the two women associated with those surnames the building represents a long line of enterprising women.

The first half of the appellation belongs to Juana Ximénez. Although the Ximénez name is generally applied to her husband Andrés Ximénez, it is Juana on whom the spotlight shines in this story. Juana Pellicer Ximénez aided in the prosperous enterprises of her husband while also giving birth to and raising five children—no small feat in any era. Unfortunately Juana died at age twenty-six, but her story lives on.

Juana Pellicer, the daughter of Minorcan native Francisco Pellicer, was born December 16, 1776, in New Smyrna, Florida. Her life began on the indigo plantation where her parents Francisco Pellicer and Margarita (nee Femanias) lived and worked as indentured servants. The plantation owner was Scotsman Dr. Andrew Turnbull who brought immigrants to the New World from the Mediterranean island of Minorca as well as from Corsica, Italy, and Greece. The purpose was to cultivate indigo plants in Florida, the newly acquired British province obtained from Spain by treaty in 1763. The peasants, struggling for subsistence in their homelands, were promised free passage to new settlements in the western hemisphere with the prospect of property ownership dangling before them as the proverbial "carrot before the donkey."

The group collectively known as Minorcans survived nine years in deplorable conditions before they rebelled in 1777. Of the fourteen hundred Mediterraneans that left from the port of Mahon, Minorca, in 1768, only about seven hundred endured the hardships. Under the leadership of Pellicer, six hundred fled New Smyrna seeking sanctuary in St. Augustine. Juana and her older brother Antonio were among the children in that trek that took them to a new home in a town where the Minorcans took refuge and the Pellicer name grew to prominence.

Early in 1780 Pellicer and fellow refugee José Peso de Burgo bought land on what is now St. George Street and together built a wooden house with a common wall separating the living quarters in which they lived comfortably for a few years.

By 1783 the family had grown and Juana had a younger brother, Bartolomé, the first child born to the family in St. Augustine, and two younger sisters, Catarina and Margarita. In addition to his house Pellicer cultivated eight and a half acres of land for which he paid rent. Life was pleasant in the St. George Street home, although disrupted during the years 1783 and 1784 as the British left Florida after twenty years of ownership and the Spanish regained possession.

The return of the Spanish was not a difficult transition for the Minorcans whose language was Spanish and who shared the Catholic faith with those resettling. It was during that period of change seven-year-old Juana's mother died. With five young children to care for, Pellicer quickly remarried. Shortly after marriage he and his second wife, Juana Villa, moved north from St. George Street to a site near present Orange Street. The following year he was listed as living on the street of the Hornabeque, a boundary along the north end of town. Records show he owned a house and lot and a female slave. In addition to his occupation as carpenter, he also farmed three acres of land.

Although an uneducated man, Pellicer did well for himself and his family. He was of strong character as reflected in his selection as the leader of the rebellion from New Smyrna. He continued as a prosperous businessman and conscientious father of a family ultimately numbering fourteen children.

Juana was too young at the time of departure from New Smyrna to remember the indigo plantation or strenuous trek to St. Augustine. Her childhood was that of a little girl in a growing family with only their own resources to rely on. They indeed came from nothing to a town with a tenuous future. The loss of her mother, though difficult for the family, was not an uncommon occurrence due to the low life expectancy of women. Undoubtedly Juana assumed numerous responsibilities as the oldest daughter in the family. Considering her father's position as a leader among the Minorcans and her own status in the family, she probably was a mature young woman in April 1791 when at age fifteen she married the merchant Andrés Ximénez.

Boarders pose outside the popular rooming house known for its longevity as a business operation run by women. The Ximénez-Fatio House today is owned and managed by the National Society of the Colonial Dames of America. (Print from author's collection)

Within a few months of their marriage Ximénez purchased a two-story wooden house on the corner of Hospital Street (now Aviles Street) and a lane later called Cadiz Street. The couple ran a store from the home located across the street from the property on which would be built the house we see today.

By 1797 the couple had prospered sufficiently to add the property across the street to their holdings. They began building on the Hospital Street site forming walls from coquina, an indigenous stone used by the Spanish, and laying tabby floors.

The result was a two-story house facing east with two single-story storerooms running westerly. A coquina kitchen with a cooking fireplace was constructed in the ample courtyard. Interpreters today believe the two front rooms (east side) were used as a general store and a tavern. Ximénez held licenses for lotteries, billiards, and alcohol, and although Juana was not named in the legal papers, she most certainly helped in the business ventures run from their home.

A second floor and an attic contained rooms for the growing family. Juana and Andrés had five children before Juana died in September

1802. By 1806 Andrés and two of the children died. The remaining three youngsters were taken by Juana's father, the now legendary Francisco Pellicer, to raise.

By 1821 Florida changed hands once again this time as a territory under the jurisdiction of the United States. As guardian of the surviving Ximénez children and executer of his son-in-law's will, Pellicer had maintained the house on Hospital Street offering it for rent, probably with some pieces of the Ximénez furniture remaining in the home. Before the changing of the flag, the property was divided into equal thirds among the Ximénez children. It stood ready for new owners when Margaret and Samuel Cook of Charleston, South Carolina, arrived shortly after United States ownership.

Although Samuel's trade had been that of tailor at the time of his marriage to Margaret in 1810, they were running a boarding house by 1813. Margaret, a widow, had one child from her former marriage, Elizabeth M. Brebner, who traveled to St. Augustine with her mother and stepfather in 1821—the year of the change of flags. Samuel immediately dabbled in business ventures in the new territory. He is listed as selling dry goods to include woolens, homespun blankets, and shawls. It is also recorded that he bought property from Pedro Miranda on April 4, 1822.[1]

However, Samuel did not remain in the picture for long. His death in 1826 left Margaret a widow, but hardly a helpless one. From 1826 to 1830 she slowly acquired the Hospital Street house and property from the Ximénez heirs, buying from each of the three children one at a time.

Margaret came to St. Augustine with ample business experience. While in Charleston with Samuel she was the "sole and separate (sic) dealer . . . in buying, selling, bartering and exchanging. . . . "[2]

It is Margaret Cook whose name is most closely associated with the establishment of a boarding house in the former Ximénez home, but it was Eliza C. Whitehurst whose quick wits and stamina guided the business.

Eliza arrived in St. Augustine in 1829 and immediately assumed the responsibilities of running the accommodations. She was a widow who brought with her a young daughter named Anna Elizabeth.

Eliza Whitehurst was hardly a stranger to Margaret Cook. Evidence analyzed from recent family research indicates Margaret and Eliza were sisters. Additionally, both Margaret and Eliza were neighbors in Charleston living on popular Tradd Street in 1819.[3]

Being a sister might have sufficed, but Margaret knew that Eliza had a reputation as a gracious hostess to travelers in Georgetown Parish,

South Carolina, near Charlotte. According to a journal written by General Peter Horry during the years 1812 to 1819, Mrs. Whitehurst provided food and lodging to notable travelers. Undoubtedly, Margaret had substantial reason to rely on Eliza to run her boarding house.

Another interesting aside regarding the Tradd Street neighborhood includes a third person, Rachel Gerty (also spelled Girty, Gherty, or Gurty) who resided on the Charleston street at the same time. Rachel came to St. Augustine in 1822 as a widow with one child and resided in the town until her death in 1863. Her friendship with Eliza and Margaret also extended to another early family in town, the Peck family (see the Woman's Exchange story).

Dr. Seth Peck had stayed at Mrs. Whitehurst's boarding house in 1833 when he was reconnoitering St. Augustine in preparation for a family relocation. When he and his wife Sarah arrived in 1834 with five children ranging in age from three to eighteen, they were ensconced in rooms in the west wing of Mrs. Whitehurst's house. The Pecks became friends with Eliza as well as Rachel Gerty and Margaret Cook.

The lives of the women became inextricably intertwined. Rachel was a charter member of the Presbyterian Church of St. Augustine founded in 1824 which Eliza, Margaret, and the Peck family later joined. Rachel eventually owned a house on St. George Street directly across from the Peck home. Next door to Sarah Peck's house was the home of John M. Hanson, the husband of Margaret Cook's daughter Elizabeth and in whose home Margaret resided.

To add to the numerous overlaps, Seth and Sarah Peck's son John attended New York University at the same time as Eliza Whitehurst's son Daniel W. Whitehurst. Daniel graduated in 1843 and John in 1844.

In 1841 Sarah joined the ranks of widowhood through which Margaret, Eliza, and Rachel were already aligned. The four women, two of them biological sisters, managed their lives and families admirably despite any obstacles.

An additional bond between sisters Margaret Cook and Eliza Whitehurst was the marriage of Eliza's daughter Anna to James M. Hanson, the brother of Elizabeth's husband John Hanson. The marriage took place around 1836 and came to an unfortunate end in April 1837 when James drowned in a shipwreck off the coast of Savannah. Six years later Anna remarried Reverend Rufus King Sewall who gained notoriety in the 1840s as "The Presbyterian Minister Who Was Run Out of Town" written about in *Florida's First Presbyterians: A Celebration of 175 years in St. Augustine, 1824–1999.*

It was during the years of ownership by Margaret Cook and management by Eliza C. Whitehurst that major renovations were made to the house resulting in the appearance seen today. Realizing the economic importance of a boarding house in the struggling yet growing community, the sisters strove to entice clientele to the Hospital Street house with their hospitality and efficiency. They were at one time leading in the competition among ten other boarding houses.

A wooden second floor and balcony were added above the two warehouses built by Ximénez. The completed remodeling provided eight rooms in the west wing, each room with its own fireplace. Attic space was increased and the outdoor kitchen doubled in size.

The front of the second story was reserved for the proprietor. Eliza Whitehurst had a large bedroom in the southeast quarter, a large parlor, and work area. Single men used small bedrooms on the ground floor, families and single women occupied space on the second floor, and overflow guests or servants used the third floor attic rooms.

Of the many boarders finding temporary sanctuary in Mrs. Whitehurst's comfortable accommodations was a woman who would become influential during the years of the Territorial Period and early statehood in St. Augustine. Clarissa C. Fairbanks boarded at Mrs. Whitehurst's while visiting her friends Dr. Andrew and Mary Anderson. That visit took place in 1832. Unknown at the time, Clarissa was to become the second Mrs. Andrew Anderson upon Mary's death and prove to be an influential figure throughout Florida's Territorial Period and into early statehood.

The Whitehurst-Cook business partnership was prospering when a series of tragedies struck. Within a year of the death of Anna's husband James in 1837, Margaret's daughter Elizabeth (Anna's cousin) died. This was followed by the death of Eliza Whitehurst in June 1838. The series of tragedies prompted Margaret Cook to sell the boarding house. On July 27, 1838, the property was purchased by another competent business woman—Sarah Petty Anderson.

Born in North Carolina but raised in the Bahamas, Sarah and her husband George arrived in Florida as the peninsula was changing hands from Spanish to American ownership. They ran a plantation on the Halifax River until his death in 1830 when Sarah sold that plantation and purchased another called Dunlawton. After it was destroyed by Seminole Indian raids Sarah relocated in St. Augustine.

With the purchase of the Hospital Street building Sarah chose to convert the structure to a private residence and fill it with numerous family members. She seemed to do well financially and, although there was great demand for boarding houses in St. Augustine, Sarah never bowed to temptation. Instead of seeking visitors for income, Sarah Anderson seemed to be land oriented. Shortly after her arrival in St. Augustine she settled accounts with Dr. Seth Peck by giving him fifty young orange trees, evidently cultivated on her out-of-town property.[4]

It was Sarah who completed the process leading to the current appearance of the house and property. She purchased the lot on Hospital Street between her house and the home of Judge Joseph Lee Smith to the north. The land and garden complement the stately structure. Sarah remained the mistress of the house until she sold it in 1855.

The second half of the double name of the Ximénez-Fatio House belongs to Louisa Fatio who successfully ran a boarding house in the building from 1855 until her death in 1875.

Louisa Fatio was the daughter of Francis Philip Fatio Jr., a wealthy property owner with holdings northwest of St. Augustine. He named his plantation along the banks of the St. Johns River New Switzerland in honor of his father's homeland. Louisa, her sister Eliza, and five half-brothers and sisters grew up in the beautiful surroundings as Florida entered into turbulent times.

Louisa was fifteen years old during the "patriot wars," the unauthorized attempt to liberate Florida from Spain for the United States. The Fatio plantation was raided and the home burned, forcing the family to flee to safer territory. The family escaped in 1812 and did not return until 1824 when Florida was in its third year of United States ownership. By then Louisa was twenty-seven years old and unmarried. After the death of the sisters' stepmother in 1828, Eliza married and moved to St. Augustine. Louisa continued to manage family affairs at New Switzerland after her father died in 1831.

The 1830s, however, was the decade of Indian warfare as the Seminoles struggled to protect their land from the encroaching Americans. An attack on the plantation in 1836 totally destroyed the family home and Louisa chose to experiment with new opportunities in St. Augustine.

After two successful business ventures running boarding houses on the bayfront and St. George Street, Louisa decided to purchase the Hospital Street house of Sarah Anderson. In May 1855 the transaction was completed and Louisa was the proud owner of her own business.

Although it was operated as a successful hostelry, Louisa's house also endured the constant patter of little feet scampering across the wooden floors as it had during the Sarah Anderson years. Louisa's sister had died but her extended family of half-sisters and brothers living with her included Sophia Fatio and four children of Leonora Fatio Colt who had died leaving the children with an irresponsible father. By 1860 she also had three nephews listed as living in her home. However, this did not deter patrons. One lodger spoke of the home-like and comfortable lodgings of Miss Fatio.[5] Her list of guests included visitors from numerous northern cities.

As the years of civil strife approached, travel ceased and visitors to St. Augustine vanished. Even so, during Union occupancy Louisa and her family appeared to do well fostered perhaps by acknowledging alliance to the United States president. They were prepared when the war ended to accept the influx of visitors flocking to the state intrigued by stories spread by soldiers who had returned home from their St. Augustine duties. It was, in fact, a boom time for the town and Louisa's well-respected rooms garnered the $15 to $20 weekly fee boarding places of that caliber charged.

One noted author attracted to Miss Fatio's house was Constance Fenimore Woolson who wove St. Augustine themes into several novels such as *Rodman the Keeper* and *East Angels*. She also wrote about life in St. Augustine during the years between the Civil War and the advent of the Golden Era of Henry M. Flagler. Woolson's visits to Louisa's house ended as the gracious hostess' health failed. Louisa Fatio died in 1875 at the age of seventy-eight.

The Fatio heirs retained the building as a boarding house but relied on outside management resulting in failing stature. Finally all property shares were turned over to Louisa's nephew David L. Dunham who in 1938 sold the house to The National Society of the Colonial Dames of America in the State of Florida. Dunham restricted the new owners from changing the appearance from its original look, a stipulation with which the Dames were in total agreement. As an organization their focus has always been toward educational enhancement for which the Fatio house qualified.

By 1979, after painstaking and thoughtful renovating, the house was opened to the public representing the 1830–1838 Territorial Period appearance—the era when Margaret Cook owned the home and Eliza C. Whitehurst ran the business.

The stories of the women within the Hospital Street walls are impressive. All endured some sort of hardship and blossomed regardless. They will be remembered:

⁘ Juana Pellicer Ximénez: A spunky sort possessing great resolve.
⁘ Margaret Cook: A resourceful and no-nonsense woman.
⁘ Eliza C. Whitehurst: An astute and conscientious hostess.

‡ Sarah Anderson Petty: A hospitable homemaker who opened her arms and hearth to family.

‡ Louisa Fatio: An elegant and astute business woman with heart.

And not to be ignored . . .

‡ The Colonial Dames: Educators with a purpose.

🌿

LUCY ABBOTT
Dream Builder (1870s–1900)

If you build it, they will come.
Lucy Abbott must have heard a version of that now classic saying from the movie "Field of Dreams" echoing in her head when she contemplated building on the unsettled land north of Colonial St. Augustine. She built "it" and "they" came making her St. Augustine's first female land developer.

"Miss Lucy," as she was called, took pristine land, parceled it out, and raised dwellings where trees once stood. She was one of a handful of builders involved in home construction outside the city limits prior to expansion during the Golden Era of millionaire Henry Morrison Flagler. Although only nine extant Abbott homes remain in the subdivision north of the city, construction is generally attributed to her with Abbott Tract representing several developed sections of property. The peak of growth in that area occurred around 1904 when 126 homes filled the lots between Fort Marion (now Castillo de San Marcos) and the Mission of Nombre de Dios.

Lucy Abbott first saw St. Augustine before the Civil War. Her words are prophetic, "My mother came to St. Augustine for her health when I was but a mere child. I almost cried my eyes out as St. Augustine was such a poor-looking place, with many small and wretched looking houses."[1]

Abbott wrote that her grandfather, Thomas Starke, moved to Spring Garden, Florida, before the Civil War and owned a large plantation along the St. Johns River. He apparently provided the impetus for Abbott's later move to the state.

Lucy Abbott was a single woman in her early thirties when she settled in St. Augustine in the 1860s. Always described as spunky and in later years bespectacled, the little dynamo began purchasing land adjacent

This sketch, penned by Zotom, a Kiowa Indian prisoner at the Castillo de San Marcos in the 1870s, depicts a house constructed by Lucy Abbott. The extant house faces Water Street and borders the fort green. (Photo courtesy of Maurine Boles)

to Fort Marion until she owned a large tract.

Land speculation north of the city was moving at a feverish pace when she arrived. New Yorker Peter Skenandoah Smith had moved to St. Augustine during the Territorial Period (1821–1845), purchasing land from Canary Islander José Noda in 1838. The land, immediately north of the fort and adjacent to the northerly dairy farm of Juan Genopoly, became a hot commodity as Smith sold lots for development.

The subdivision extended from Clinch Street, now the northern strip of the Fort Green, northward to Joiner Street. The eastern boundary was the marshland overlooking Matanzas Bay. To the west was Shell Road now San Marco Avenue.

Her uncle, Captain John W. Starke, who built a house on the corner of Water and Shenandoah Streets around 1861, aided Miss Lucy's ventures. That house later became Miss Abbott's primary residence while she constructed homes between 1872 and 1894, nine of which are still extant. She was living in the Water Street house at the time of her death on October 29, 1929, the day of the stock market crash. The astute businesswoman did not witness the oncoming decade of the Great Depression.

Perhaps the most impressive of Abbott's accomplishments is the three-story Colonial Revival building at 14 Joiner Street constructed between 1872 and 1885. At first topped by a Mansard roof, a French style typified by two slopes on each of the four sides, the house was later modified to its current Colonial look. The Mansard roof was removed and a two-story portico supported by massive round columns replaced an open porch. Now lost behind a thicket of trees and obscured by houses, Abbott Mansion and the castle-like Moorish Revival home of oil millionaire William G. Warden once dominated the view looking north from the City Gate. Abbott Mansion is now a bed and breakfast called The Mansion. Castle Warden is the home of the original *Ripley's Believe It or Not!* Museum collection.

Over the years, Miss Lucy must have taken great pride in strolling the streets of the rapidly growing neighborhood watching her houses rise above the land to become the homes of numerous prosperous residents. Those homeowners included Charles Floyd Hopkins, a descendant of Indian Agent Gad Humphreys and his wife Isabella Gibbs Hopkins, a descendent of Confederate Army Colonel George Couper Gibbs.

In addition to the mansion and a smaller house west of it on Joiner Street, Miss Abbott constructed a row of houses along the river-lined strip of Water Street. The houses, generally typified by commodious two-story porches, neo-classical balustrades, and wood-scroll trim, remain elegant reminders of the ambition and foresight of the lady from South Carolina.

Although little has been written about Lucy Abbott, it is evident from her own words she was an observant analyst of human behavior. She wrote about the pavilion in the Plaza de la Constitución referring to it as the "meat market." The market, sometimes referred to as a "slave market," is occasionally a controversial topic. She said, "The meat market was erected by the city in the Plaza, and when the top was burned off the weather vane, a brass beef, was secured by a colored man and sold for five dollars . . . I have this (on) authority from Mr. Venancio Sanchez whose slaves were being divided among the heirs outside of the meat market. A heavy rain coming up, they went inside of the market. Slaves were never sold there."

She continues with her explanation of the recurring debate about the old market. "A Mr. Leighton, the photographer who had a studio near the City Gates (sic) was the first one to call it a slave market, thinking the photoes (sic) would sell more readily by so doing."

She specifically clarifies her observations by writing, "I am talking about what I saw before the war."

Miss Lucy was a staunch supporter of the Confederacy and is credited with aiding in the erection of the monument in the Plaza de la Constitución honoring the Confederate soldiers who died fighting for the South.

But that is not all the spunky, bespeckled dreamer did. She brought pleasure to many through her musical talents as demonstrated during fifteen years as organist of Trinity Parish Episcopal Church. The little woman playing the hymns on Sunday was in sharp contrast to the business contractor overseeing the construction of houses.

Lucy Abbot was the first female real estate entrepreneur in St. Augustine. She "almost cried her eyes out" when she first saw the small and wretched houses of the old town. So she changed that image by becoming not just a homebuilder, but also a builder of dreams.

LUELLA DAY McCONNELL
Diamond Lil's Outrageous Tourism Venture (1900s)

I have not got Insanity.
I have not got Hysteria.
And I have not got any Ladylike complications.

Those are the words spoken by Luella Day McConnell in a speech given to the St. Augustine Tourist Club in January 1909.[1]

That's what she didn't have. What she did have was a generous portion of guile mixed with Barnum and Bailey bravado, and a dash of ladylike charm. The result bought her a ticket through the front door to some exotic places and propelled her into proprietorship of a major tourist attraction in the nation's oldest city—the Fountain of Youth.

Luella Day McConnell was by all accounts a flamboyant extremist who twirled the world around her head like a lasso curled for the throw. She posed coyly for her self-published book *The Tragedy of the Klondike*, stating on the title page, "This book of travels gives the *true facts* of what took place in the gold-fields under British Rule." Facts by definition are statements proven to be true. Most of her "facts" were not.

As a single woman in her mid-twenties, Luella Day was attracted to the Klondike during the outbreak of gold-rush fever that descended on the United States in 1897. Her adventurous spirit and outlandish imagination made a name for her in the Klondike then and still sparks interest now, a century later.

In 1950 Frederick W. Benson wrote to the St. Augustine Historical Society with information substantiating some facts printed by McConnell and debunking others. Though he never met McConnell, he had lived in the Klondike, a region of Canada's Yukon Territory, from 1906 to 1909 as an employee of the Canadian Bank of Commerce and he felt qualified to refute her claims. He arrived in the northern post of Dawson, Yukon Territory, shortly after McConnell's departure and became friends with people characterized in her book, thus his motivation to correct her grievances.

In a gentle, condescending style Benson begins, "The early part of the book appears to be fairly accurate. She made the trip to Skagway, Alaska, on the S.S. *Islander*. I also made a trip on the same ship in the following year, 1899."

After establishing his own credibility and suggesting an unbiased report, he changes his tone by writing:

> *Starting about page 72 the author begins to get away from the truth. She refers to many men by name and accuses them of terrible things, including theft, extortion and even attempted or actual murders . . . Their fine record is too well known to be damaged by the writings of a woman, who, to be charitable, I must consider as having been mentally unbalanced.*

About this time the author warms to the subject and tells Marian Moulds, the librarian of Webb Memorial Library to whom the letter is addressed, what he really thinks of Diamond Lil.

> *The writer of the book undoubtedly magnifies her importance. She was probably a meddlesom [sic] person with a complex of self-pity and the book was no doubt written in a spirit of spite, perhaps because she could not have her own way in everything. If she had been one-half as important as she makes out, I certainly would have heard more about her. In fact, I recall only hearing some brief references to 'Diamond Lil' and did not even know her proper name until I read the book a few days ago.[2]*

Many years later in 1978 Ian Whitaker, a Canadian anthropology professor, discovered McConnell's book and noted it contained a picture of her house in St. Augustine thus prompting him to write the historical society for more information about her. He wanted to include her in a "Who's Who" of the Klondike, but could not justify her importance from what she wrote. He questioned her credibility as a physician and then suggested she was "suffering from a serious paranoia condition." He claimed she was charged with criminal libel after verbal attacks on government officials. Moreover, he said attempts on her life ultimately caused her to escape from Dawson by fleeing downstream along the Klondike River in 1903.[3]

In *Klondike Women* Melanie Mayer is kinder to McConnell giving her credit for medical training. According to Mayer's account Luella Day practiced medicine in Dawson until the Canadian physicians organized and required all doctors to be registered. Certification meant passing a medical exam which could only be taken upon proof of completion of a four-year medical course. Luella either could not or did not want to produce such evidence and elected to practice medicine in the capacity of a nurse.

During her years in the Klondike, a handsome and prosperous adventurer arrived in Dawson and captured her interest. Tall, red-haired Edward McConnell was a miner who owned a steamboat and operated a ferry across the Klondike River. The two married on September 26, 1898. Luella Day McConnell was approximately twenty-eight years old. (She is believed to have been born around 1870 in Baltimore, Maryland.)

When her exploits forced her withdrawal from the Klondike and sent her in search of new excitement, she left the frozen north for the sizzling south. She had a diamond set in one of her front teeth earning her the nickname of "Diamond Lil." That nickname was just a ripple in the stream of names she accumulated over time. She was called Luella Day, Louella Day, MD, Luella McConnell, Lyonell M. Day, and Lyonella Murat Day. The Murat appellation came from her claim to be a member of the Napoleon Bonaparte family. A nephew of the emperor Prince Napoleon Achille Murat lived for a time in St. Augustine. The St. Bernard McConnell owned while in the Yukon was named Napoleon.

When Diamond Lil arrived in St. Augustine in 1900 with her husband, her appearance drew raves. And if the diamond in her tooth didn't dazzle them, the rings on her fingers certainly did. She tossed her ermine wrap across a chair in the lavish Hotel Ponce de León dining room like the "Unsinkable" Molly Brown at the captain's table on the *Titanic*—but without Molly's savoir faire.

Luella Day McConnell strikes a saucy pose in a photo used in her self-published book: The Tragedies of the Klondike. *(Photo from the St. Augustine Historical Society)*

Residents were impressed and the local society column in the *Tatler* on January 27, 1900, reported Mrs. McConnell to be "a lady of rare beauty and gracefulness" who was worth all the gold in the Yukon.

No doubt Diamond Lil was a charmer and no doubt she had money. In short order the McConnells purchased a substantial parcel of land north of the city. The acquisition included a house built in 1869 by Henry H. Williams who ran a successful produce business supplying fruits and vegetables to hotels and markets in the city. Of little significance at the time was the presence on the property of a "flowing well surrounded by a square coquina wall on four sides." That description written by A. T. Monteau in 1880 preceded any reference to a "fountain of youth." Mention was also made of the discovery of human bones on the property that Williams promptly reinterred out of respect for the dead. Before the McConnells had time to settle in, they promptly disappeared leaving the property and two dogs (one a St. Bernard—perhaps Napoleon) in the care of a groundskeeper.[4]

It is difficult to know at this point exactly where to sort through the myth and legends. It was believed Edward McConnell had drowned shortly after leaving St. Augustine—or did he? They both lost money— or did they? She found Spanish documents to prove the landing of Ponce de León on the very property she had purchased—or did she?

The rumors of Edward McConnell's death were definitely exaggerated. He didn't drown in the Yukon—he showed up again in St. Augustine in 1902. Then after another disappearance in the 1920s he suddenly surfaced to claim his inheritance after Luella died.

Luella probably did lose the money she apparently acquired before she first arrived in St. Augustine. She returned after a two-year hiatus without the diamonds and ermine. It was then she began selling water from the alleged fountain of youth for ten cents a glass. She built an archway over the property entrance and began charging admission to the newly labeled park grounds. Her claims included the assertion that the Chinese built a fort there that Ponce de León completed when he landed. She also did the unbelievable (although most of what she did was unbelievable) by advertising for German colonists to settle on her property. That was at the onset of the Great War (World War I). According to a document written by Emily L. Wilson, a wireless radio was found on the premises and McConnell was temporarily jailed for the escapade.

Emily Wilson was a scholarly woman and a valuable asset at the time to the fledgling historical society. She was the great-niece of John L. Wilson who gave the Public Library Building to the city of St. Augustine. She herself contributed tirelessly by providing well-documented research papers to the society. She had questioned the location of the arrival of Ponce de León long before the famous Fountain of Youth became a tourist attraction. Wilson also offered the most interesting descriptions of Luella and her exploits.

Wilson was twenty-three years old when she made her first visit to St. Augustine in 1892. In 1900 she returned to Florida in the hopes of improving her failing health. While here she heard rumors from Captain

Henry and Mrs. Marcotte, social commentators of the time, that a wealthy couple had arrived from the Klondike and wanted to buy the Williams estate. There was also talk that the woman had a diamond imbedded in her front tooth and possessed an ermine cloak. Wilson and her sister were in the Ponce de León Hotel when the McConnells arrived for dinner. She wrote, "It was the days of black silk, fur-lined cloaks and Mrs. McConnell spread hers over the back of her chair, setting on it, showing all the ermine and she put both her hands on the railing and there were rings with jewels on every finger of both hands." She further describes Luella as "a tall slender woman, rather pretty, black hair."

The charitable description belies her distrust of the woman who Miss Wilson later discredited. Indeed, Miss Wilson worked diligently to disprove the myth that Ponce de León landed on St. Augustine's shores, discovered a fountain of youth and laid stones in the form of a cross with fifteen stones forming the stanchion and thirteen creating the arms. The numbers were said to indicate the year, 1513, that Ponce de León trod upon the marshland north of the later Spanish settlement of St. Augustine.

In 1909 the *St. Augustine Record* lauded the discovery of the cross on the McConnell grounds, the reporter gullibly believing the tale that the cross made of the indigenous coquina stone had been unearthed on the property. Also found buried in the ground was a metal casket containing parchment paper with instructions regarding its placement. The article maintains that the cross is "undoubtedly a genuine relic of the earliest date in St. Augustine's history. . . ."[5]

Wilson pored over documents found in the Library of Congress in Washington, D.C., to determine the authenticity of the claims and found McConnell's own additions to the collection of historic records. Incredulous about the successful scam Miss Wilson later tried to dissuade Walter Fraser from purchasing the property and claiming it was the authentic "fountain of youth." Her pleas went unheeded then and now. To this day Luella Day McConnell's claims are flaunted before the tourists who flock to the Ancient City eager to see the Fountain of Youth where Ponce de León landed and found magical waters.

Her foray into St. Augustine and perpetuation of the fountain of youth myth did not buy longevity for the woman who felt she could do anything. She was killed in a car accident on Thursday, June 23, 1927, near Ocala, Florida. In death as in life she made headlines.

The *St. Augustine Record* referred to her as Mrs. Lyonella Murat Day. She had divorced her husband at least ten years before her death although she frequently claimed he was dead. Why the spelling change in her first name remains a mystery. Apparently she preferred the Mrs. title to Miss even though she combined the married title with her maiden name. The use of Murat as a middle name is not unusual considering her position in St. Augustine where the Prince Murat Tea and Coffee House was becoming a popular gathering place and included a visit in 1939 by actress Greta Garbo.

She was not driving the car in which she died. Her friend Katherine H. Carefoot of Jacksonville, Florida, was at the wheel and apparently lost control while attempting to pass another vehicle. The car careened into a ditch killing Luella instantly. Her companion succumbed several days later. Luella died with no diamonds other than the one imbedded in her front tooth.

Controversy began immediately upon word of her death. The estate of Lyonella Murat Day was bequeathed to her brother-in-law John McConnell, a blind man living in Hanford, California. That will was dated 1922 and named the executor as lawyer Helen Hunt West, formerly of St. Augustine and a proponent of women's rights. Her former husband, Edward McConnell, very much alive, appeared with a will dated 1901 and signed by Luella Day McConnell. The controversial fire fizzled when John McConnell relinquished all claim to the estate. The details, however, remained to be sorted through.

Meanwhile, Walter B. Fraser, businessman, community leader and a state senator in the 1940s, obtained permits and began renovation of the structure on the Fountain of Youth property. Fraser and his wife laid claim to the property through association with the Ponce de León Fountain of Youth Company. Fraser claimed ownership through a warranty deed issued to him from the Ponce de León Fountain of Youth Company. Apparently the property had been incorporated by Louella D. McConnell as early as 1919. Once the dust settled the property was in the hands of Fraser who already was enlarging on its popularity as a significant tourist attraction.

Adding to the confusion was the discovery of numerous art objects to include paintings purported to be originals by Rembrandt and Raphael. Luella had indeed muddied the waters even in death. The claims were eventually settled and the Fountain of Youth tourist attraction continued under the ownership and direction of the Fraser family. Luella's imaginary fountain to this day attracts the curious.

It is believed that Diamond Lil was the model for the poem by Robert W. Service, "The Lady That's Known as Lou." However, opinions about the eccentric Luella varied. Some admired her spunk but not everyone thought kindly of her. In his 1950 letter to Marian Moulds, Frederic W. Benson said, "Some people may wonder why she was not sued for libel and slander by a number of people. It may be that they felt that this would be playing into her hands and give her a lot of publicity. Sometimes it is better to ignore persons of this sort and let them die off in obscurity."

Diamond Lil with all of her aliases did not die off in obscurity. She made her mark and left an indelible imprint in St. Augustine and possibly in the Klondike as well.

As for the Fountain of Youth, significant strides have been taken to give the historic piece of property the respect it deserves. It was the village of Seloy, home to the Timucuan Indians, when Pedro Menendéz founded St. Augustine in 1565.

Archeological excavations under the direction of Dr. Kathleen Deagan of the University of Florida continue to produce evidence of the Indian village and the early Spanish settlement. A new exhibit housed on the property presents a precise time line of the history of the land.[6] It also explains the skeletal remains that were found by Williams in 1880. The bones he buried were found again in 1934 by a gardener. In 1952 the Timucuan Indian remains were put on exhibit in a low-ceilinged building with an observation deck. After years of display followed by increased pressure for proper respect, the remains were reburied with a Catholic consecration service and a Native American ceremony in 1991.[7]

Emily Wilson, vociferous opponent to Diamond Lil's outrageous tourist venture said, "There is no fountain of youth as we all know, and it is silly and quacky to carry on the inventions of a woman who was not in her right mind."[8]

It is easy enough to say Luella Day McConnell was not in her right mind. However, she managed to carry her name into perpetuity sane or not. And if it was her intention to draw people here to drink the mystical waters recapturing youth, that is no more harmful than kissing the Blarney Stone to achieve magical eloquence.

Her claims regarding the landing of Ponce de León have no historic or archeological proof. Few people are fooled by the carefully constructed stone cross marking the date of 1513. And perhaps some day those misconceptions will be rectified.

Luella Day McConnell, also known as Diamond Lil, perpetuated a myth that still entices tourists to the nation's oldest city. Real or fabled, it accomplished the purpose of a woman determined to leave her mark on the world.

CHAPTER VI

Flagler's Women

❧

WOMEN INFLUENTIAL IN A MILLIONAIRE'S LIFE
(1840s–1930s)

Henry Morrison Flagler (1830–1913), a multimillionaire, co-partner in Standard Oil Company, and Florida's uncrowned king, was by most accounts a self-made man. He grew up in humble surroundings, the son of an itinerant Presbyterian minister who supported his family primarily with money acquired from farming. His childhood of near poverty fanned his ambition to become wealthy, and was a driving force in his quest for money and power. Although confident in his aspirations, he was guided in his early years both by the practical advice of experienced relatives and business partners, and also by the gentle touch bestowed on him by the women in his family. In his later years, as a multimillionaire oil tycoon, he was equally touched by women; however, this time by far stronger persuasions from his female companions.

The women influencing Henry Flagler's life from childhood to beyond the grave were Elizabeth, Anne Caroline "Carrie," Mary, Jennie Louise, Ida Alice, Mary Lily, and Louise.

ELIZABETH
Elizabeth Caldwell Morrison Flagler

Leading the list is Elizabeth Caldwell Morrison, Henry's mother, who played a considerable role in his future success. Elizabeth married Isaac Flagler in 1828. Isaac had a daughter, Anne Caroline "Carrie" Flagler, from a previous marriage and Elizabeth brought with her a son, Daniel Morrison Harkness. Henry was their only child together. Dan, Carrie, and Henry grew up in the same household with Henry admiring his older brother and adoring his big sister.

As a child, Henry was exposed daily to the ministry. His father repeatedly urged him to pursue religious work and farming, professions Henry adamantly rejected. Elizabeth understood her son's need to explore other options and helped Henry become established with successful business owners from the Harkness side of the family. Elizabeth was the widow of David Harkness, the father of Henry's half brother, Dan.

In 1838 Dan set out from his Toledo, Ohio, home to work with Harkness family members in and around Bellevue, Ohio. The following year Elizabeth moved with Carrie and Henry to Medina, New York. Although Isaac had answered a call from a nearby Presbyterian church, he was away from home much of the time pursuing missionary work. Elizabeth was ostensibly left alone to care for Carrie and Henry. Dan and Henry corresponded during this time and Elizabeth became ever aware of her younger son's desire to follow her eldest into the business world. At age fourteen, Henry received permission from his mother to leave school and travel to his half brother who was employed by his Uncle Lamon's mercantile firm in a branch store in Republic, Ohio. Although the departure must have been bittersweet for mother and son, it was the path to success for Henry.

Henry's trek into Ohio in 1844 ended at the store in Republic managed by Dan Harkness as part of the Harkness family business interests. Henry's meager finances consisted of a five-cent piece, four pennies, and a five-franc piece he kept as a memento throughout his life. The franc represented to him the Biblical tale of the man who had but one talent, perhaps representing Flagler's desire to take risks in order to achieve success.[1]

Although Dan and Henry initially struggled, they proved themselves to be conscientious and astute businessmen. As they both were woven into the family business fabric, their social lives evolved into even stronger ties. In 1849 Dan married Lamon's oldest daughter, Isabella. The following year, 1853, Henry intertwined the bonds even tighter when he married Lamon's second daughter, Mary. By that time Dan had acquired Chapman, Harkness and Company and reorganized it as D. M. Harkness and Company including his uncle Lamon and half brother Henry as partners.

The close-knit families continued to prosper and welcomed the birth of Henry and Mary's first child, Jennie Louise born in 1855.

Never losing touch with his immediate family, Henry welcomed his parents and half sister Carrie when they moved to Bellevue around 1858 to be nearer to him. Isaac, who had continued his peripatetic lifestyle, was in ill health needing frequent care. Henry and Mary's second child,

Carrie, had been born in June of that year. Certainly Elizabeth was grateful not only to be in the company of her son and daughter-in-law, but also to be near her grandchildren Jennie Louise and baby Carrie.

Only a few years later, in 1861, Elizabeth was taken ill and died. Henry's devotion to his mother and his grief over her death were reflected in the tasteful funeral he organized for her and the extensive burial arrangements he made, buying a brick vault for her final resting place. No such care was bestowed on his father at his death fifteen years later. Little is known of their relationship after Elizabeth's death except that Isaac did visit the family home in Cleveland, and was present the year of the birth of Henry's son Henry "Harry" Harkness in 1870.

Elizabeth was a loving and caring mother. When Henry chose to leave school after eighth grade to seek his fortune, it was Elizabeth who gave him permission to follow his dreams. She stoically waved goodbye from the porch of their country home as fourteen-year-old Henry walked down a dirt path heading toward an unknown future. She had faith in her son and it proved to be well founded.

CARRIE
*Anne Caroline "Carrie" Flagler**

Carrie was the daughter of Isaac Flagler and his second wife, Ruth Deyo Smith. Ruth died when Carrie was seventeen months old and, a year later, Isaac married Elizabeth Harkness who brought her son Dan into the family. Carrie grew up with Henry as her younger playmate and she apparently enjoyed the role of big sister. The two remained close and Carrie, who never married, came to live with her brother Henry after his first wife Mary died in 1881. It was Carrie's job to care for Henry's son, Harry, who was ten years old at the time of his mother's death. Carrie remained part of the household with Jennie Louise, married by then, sharing some of the duties. In 1883, when Henry married Ida Alice Shourds, his late wife's caretaker, Carrie felt her duties were completed and, much to the consternation of young Harry, departed. Neither Carrie nor Harry felt any affection toward the new woman in Henry's life.

After vacationing in Europe for a few months, Carrie found an apartment of her own in Manhattan. She lived to be ninety years old, dying in 1917, four years after the death of her famous half brother Henry.

*Also listed as Ann Caroline, Anna Caroline, or Caroline.

MARY

Mary Harkness Flagler

No woman touched Henry Flagler's life as profoundly as Mary Harkness. She was his first love and a lasting love. She brought him joy and stability and was the mother of his children. In the end, however, she left him with a burden of guilt.

Henry met Mary at the Bellevue, Ohio, home of Lamon Harkness, the uncle of his half brother Dan Morrison Harkness. Dan and Henry were business partners in a mercantile venture, one of several companies owned by Lamon. Dan was dating Lamon's oldest daughter, Isabella. Dan and Isabella, though first cousins, married in 1849. After their marriage Henry continued to visit the Harkness home expressing an interest in Mary, Lamon's second daughter. Mary was only fifteen and Henry nineteen when they met and, at first, their time together consisted of platonic socialization, not courting. Mary, attractive and charming, soon came to mean more than a family friend to Henry, and the teenage friendship turned to mature love. The couple married November 9, 1853, with the blessings of Harkness and Flagler relatives.

Henry and Dan continued to work together as partners in the Bellevue firm which, during the 1850s, reaped substantial profits from whiskey sales. Henry's wealth was growing as was his family. The first born, Jennie Louise, entered the world March 18, 1855. The year 1858 marked the birth of their second child Carrie named for Henry's beloved half sister. The year's riches also provided impetus for moving to a fashionable house in Bellevue. It was the decade of the 1850s when Henry Flagler met John D. Rockefeller who, though nine years his junior, would later work with Flagler to garner fortunes through the oil industry.

Surrounded by family and friends, Mary and Henry were content with their lives. Mary's sister, Isabella, and Henry's half brother Dan, were both family and friends to them. In 1858 Henry's mother and father moved to Bellevue to be near their son bringing Henry's half sister Carrie with them. The families were together, business was prospering, and Henry felt far from the Civil War that was threatening the country.

Life was good for Mary and Henry—that is until 1861. During that year Henry's mother Elizabeth died. Then in December little three-year-old Carrie, who had been frail since birth, gave up her struggle. The loss of Elizabeth was difficult for Henry, but the death of Carrie was devastating to both her parents. Henry reacted by increasing his workload, including plans to shift his business interests. Mary, however, was despondent and her fragile health declined. Although her physical well being was of concern to her husband, he nevertheless continued with plans to sell his business and form a partnership with his newly acquired brother-in-law Barney York. York, already a business partner, had married into the family taking Mary's younger sister Julia as his bride in 1863. Pursuing success in the rapidly expanding salt business, Flagler and York moved to Saginaw, Michigan, in 1862. Mary, though not in good health, maintained a jovial attitude and enjoyed the company of her younger sister Julia, her closest companion in unfamiliar surroundings.

The first two years in the salt business were productive to the brothers-in-law. Both, however, lacked experience in the industry and competition licked away at their profits. Disaster struck after the Civil War when salt prices plummeted and the business crashed. It was the first—and only—time Henry Flagler found himself bankrupt. Putting the failure behind him Henry was determined to find wealth elsewhere. Mary and the Harkness family tried to persuade him to return to Bellevue, but Flagler had other ideas. He saw Cleveland, situated on the banks of Lake Erie and the hub of railroad and shipping routes, as a land of opportunity. He and the family moved into modest quarters as Flagler inched his way up the ladder of success. His first ventures in the grain business were disappointing, but his reputation as an ambitious businessman gained him entry into the firm of Clark and Sanford. The position he took filled a void left by John D. Rockefeller who left the grain business in pursuit of success in the petroleum industry.

Flagler was achieving success with Clark and Sanford and during these years renewed his friendship with Rockefeller. The two men worked in the same office building and often walked to and from their homes together. They frequently reminisced about the days they both were in the grain business and, although Flagler was doing well, Rockefeller looked forward, motivated by escalating oil demands and anticipating greater success in his ventures.

Rockefeller continued to expand his business including his brother William as a partner along with Englishman Samuel Andrews. By 1866, Rockefeller approached Flagler with the idea of investing in the expansion of the oil business. Flagler recommended an in-law, Stephen Harkness, as a potential investor. Stephen was the son of Lamon's brother David, making him a half brother of Dan's but was no relation to Henry. Rockefeller countered Flagler's offer by saying he would agree only if Flagler would control the money. Flagler concurred and within a short time the company's growth expanded and diversified. The company of Rockefeller, Andrews and Flagler was formed in 1867 and was to become the leader in the petroleum industry. That same year Flagler moved Mary and the children to a large house on Euclid Avenue, the most prestigious street in Cleveland.

By 1869 the partners agreed to incorporate the business as the Standard Oil Company. It became a legal entity on January 11, 1870. The idea to incorporate was Flagler's and was another step in the quest both Flagler and Rockefeller pursued for even more wealth. All but a fraction of the stock in the corporation was held by John D. Rockefeller, Stephen Harkness, Henry Flagler, Samuel Andrews, and William Rockefeller.

On December 2, 1870, less than a year from the date of incorporation, Mary gave birth to a third child, a son named Henry "Harry" Harkness Flagler. The joyous occasion was dampened by Mary's continued failing health and Flagler's focus on business concerns. Although he kept his promise to be by Mary's side every night, he was driven daily by his passion to achieve financial power.

With the rapid growth of the corporation, change was necessary and Flagler chose to move to New York, the largest city in the United States and one destined to become the financial center of the country. In 1877 the family moved into the Buckingham Hotel at the same time maintaining their home in Cleveland. Mary's chronic bronchitis was taking its toll and doctors repeatedly advised Flagler to take her to Florida for the winter months. Finally Flagler arranged a trip in December 1877, with plans to extend the retreat over several months. Harry, Jennie Louise and her husband John Hinckley went with them. Due to poor transportation, the family never traveled beyond Jacksonville with the exception of a one-day trip to St. Augustine, a sleepy town Flagler found repugnant at the time. While in Jacksonville Flagler became extremely nervous about business matters and felt compelled to return to New York. Mary refused to stay behind in Florida and she and the family traveled back with Flagler. Although physicians continued to stress the need for Mary to remain in a warm climate, Flagler was far too busy to leave his business for any length of time, and Mary was adamant about not traveling alone. On December 11, 1880, Mary's father Lamon Harkness died in the Flagler home in Cleveland. On the trip to the funeral Flagler realized there was no hope left for his beloved Mary. To make her last days comfortable, he hired Ida Alice Shourds as a companion for Mary, but it was too late. Mary died May 18, 1881.

Mary's death was a turning point in Henry's life. The man who was driven to make fortunes discovered money could not fill the deep void in his life. His lifestyle changed abruptly with marked differences in his attitude toward work as well as social life. Slowly he found a different focus. Mary's life with Henry, and her death, left indelible marks on the multimillionaire who ultimately would learn that giving money was as important as earning it.

JENNIE LOUISE

Jennie Louise Flagler Hinckley Benedict

As the first-born child, Jennie Louise immediately enriched the lives of Mary and Henry Flagler. She was born March 18, 1855, in Bellevue, Ohio, during a time the family was prospering. Three years later baby sister Carrie was born. Jennie was only six when young Carrie died and barely seven when the family moved from Bellevue, the only home she knew, to Saginaw, Michigan. Though only a child she must have carried emotional scars from the death of her sister while adjusting to a new life in a new town. Mary's health was fragile and Henry was having a difficult time with the new business in the salt industry. Jennie, however, had a safe and secure home with her mother always nearby and her father, not only at home with the family every night, but also a leader in church activities, particularly Sunday School which involved young Jennie. Flagler's failure in the salt industry never intruded on her happiness.

From Saginaw the family moved to Cleveland, Ohio, where Flagler's successful rise in business must have influenced the maturing Jennie whose status in life was above average. In 1870, when she was fifteen years old, she welcomed her baby brother Harry into the family. Although her mother's health was ever declining and her father's business increasingly kept him away from home, Jennie Louise was becoming a happy, self-confident adult.

She met and married John Arthur Hinckley April 26, 1876, at twenty-one years of age. Her new husband was quickly incorporated into the Standard Oil System by his influential father-in-law. Jennie Louise and John settled in an apartment in New York soon to be followed to the city by the rest of the Flagler family. Living nearby Jennie watched as her mother grew weaker and her father richer. She was relieved when her father finally concurred with the doctor's orders to take Mary to Florida. Jennie and John accompanied them; however, Jennie Louise's marriage was slowly deteriorating, as was Mary's health.

In March 1887, six years after her mother's death, Jennie Louise divorced Hinckley on grounds of adultery. They had been married eleven years and had no children. She may have already selected her future mate as she married Frederick H. Benedict just seven months later.

In February 1889 Flagler rejoiced at the news his daughter had given birth to a baby girl named Margery. At the suggestion of Dr. George Shelton, the physician caring for Jennie Louise, it was decided she should travel to Florida where she could recuperate in the salubrious weather and with the exceptional care her father could provide.

Benedict procured his father's yacht, the *Oneida,* determining a voyage over the water would be more easily tolerated than the trip by rail, even in Flagler's private car. Unfortunately, nothing could save Jennie Louise. Flagler reached Charleston, South Carolina, just as the *Oneida* sailed into the harbor. He quickly boarded the vessel only to find his daughter lying dead in her cabin. His happiness dissolved into grief as he learned of the death of the baby and Jennie Louise's demise from childbirth fever. Her body immediately was taken back to New York where she was buried in Woodlawn Cemetery.

Mary's death had been traumatic to Flagler and, driven by guilt over prioritizing his work ethic above her health concerns, he had ventured forth into a different lifestyle—building and giving to the community rather than following his myopic vision of increased wealth. The death of his daughter was a blow that came at a time when his St. Augustine projects were flourishing and his future beckoned. He was heartsick and for his own sake as well as for Jennie and the family, he needed a way to express his great love for his daughter. He looked around at what was becoming his Gilded-Age realm and decided to honor Jennie Louise with a glorious structure that would express not only his love for her, but also his deep religious convictions generally kept hidden from the public. His answer was to build a memorial church to be used by the local Presbyterian congregation and seen by all who visited the little Spanish town of St. Augustine he had awakened with his Midas touch.

He commissioned his architects, the youthful team of John Carrère and Thomas Hastings, to design the living memorial. The duo had created the elegant Ponce de León Hotel as well as other prestigious structures, generally displaying a Spanish Renaissance motif. Using their creativity to fashion a sanctuary elegant enough to stand proudly beside Flagler's majestic hotels, they designed a building in Venetian Renaissance style. Some of the architectural plans were patterned after the Cathedral of St. Mark's in Venice. However, they incorporated their own ideas applying Byzantine, Romanesque, Greek, and Gothic touches to the unique structure.

As Flagler requested, the church was completed in one year. The dedication ceremony took place on March 16, 1890. Tribute was paid to Jennie Louise Flagler Benedict with dignitaries from all over the country attending. Pastor John R. Paxton, from Flagler's church in New York,

Jennie Louise Flagler, daughter of Henry M. Flagler. (Photo courtesy Memorial Presby-terian Church)

conducted the service fully understanding Flagler's grief over the loss of his daughter.

Memorial gifts to Jennie Louise included the baptismal font of Siena marble presented by her husband, Frederick H. Benedict. Also her physician, Dr. George G. Shelton, gave in her memory an immense Bible with a leather binding and silver ornamentation. Both the font, which serves also as a communion table, and the Bible remain in use today in the Memorial Presbyterian Church.

Jennie Louise, with baby Margery in her arms, was entombed in the mausoleum constructed later as a final resting place for her, her mother Mary, and her father.

Flagler achieved his goal. The glorious sanctuary is a living memorial to his daughter and to the glory of God as he wished. It is the place of worship of a large Presbyterian congregation and is viewed by visitors awestruck by its magnificent beauty.

IDA ALICE
Ida Alice Shourds Flagler

Ida Alice Shourds was a child of a poor family. Like Flagler, she was mesmerized by money. Unlike Flagler, who liked to earn it, Ida Alice liked to spend it. Hired as a companion during the last months of Flagler's first wife Mary's life, Ida Alice saw how the ultrarich lived. The red-haired, blue-eyed aspiring actress caught Flagler's attention. Shortly after Mary's death Flagler purchased a sumptuous manor at Mamaroneck on the point of Long Island, New York. Named Satan's Toe, the mansion was a forty-room "summer cottage" in which the Flagler family, including half sister Carrie Flagler who came to care for Flagler's son Harry, was installed. Flagler slowly distanced himself from Standard Oil duties and began a public social life that included Ida Alice.

By June 5, 1883, Henry and Ida Alice were married, much to the dismay of family members. Carrie, who had cared for Harry for two years, left the Mamaroneck home; twelve-year-old Harry firmly refused to accept his new stepmother. The unexpected wedding was either poorly planned, or cunningly propelled by Ida Alice. June was a busy month for the oil industry and Flagler was unable to leave for a honeymoon. Although he was staunchly Presbyterian and Ida Alice was the daughter of an Episcopal minister, the wedding was held in a Methodist Church. Possibly it was the most easily accessible religious facility available on short notice. A further indication that it was a rushed event was the appearance of Ida Alice's belongings at the New York City Fifth Avenue home, the home where Mary had died and was now occupied by Flagler while in town. The trunks arrived the day after the wedding. Apparently arrangements had not been made to send her personal items to the summer home at Mamaroneck, by then called Lawn Beach rather than Satan's Toe, a name that may have been offensive to the son of a Presbyterian minister.

Several months after the wedding the honeymoon finally transpired when Flagler took his new bride, whom he called Alice, to Florida. He was lured back to the frontier land by news of enormous growth and financial profit. Although his memories of Florida from his abbreviated trip with Mary were not pleasant, nonetheless he felt compelled to revisit the primitive land. The honeymooning couple stayed from December 1883 to March 1884, spending most of their time in St. Augustine. They were fond enough of the quaint town to plan another trip a year later, returning in February 1885. Much had changed since the previous visit. The grand San Marco Hotel had been built across from the intriguing old fort. People visiting the town were not the consumptives Flagler remembered from past visits, but wealthier people eager to enjoy the balmy climate in a unique town. It was then that Flagler fully realized his dream of turning St. Augustine into the winter Newport of the South. The jewel in the crown was to be the magnificent Ponce de León Hotel which he hoped would draw the wealthy from the north. He began his plans in earnest while Alice contemplated her future as a socialite in the new environment. Her attempts toward achieving social recognition in New York had faltered despite her ambitious endeavors to become one of the admired few. Her extravagant clothing and jewels were overshadowed by her lack of social graces and occasional flares of temper. Her behavior in public, though criticized by many, was dutifully accepted by her husband.

In January 1888 the Ponce de León Hotel opened its doors to America's rich and famous. Alice was in her glory. Away from the snobbery surrounding her in New York, in St. Augustine she felt like a queen in command of the aristocracy. Unfortunately that was only her perception as the upper class looked down on her and no amount of expensive luxuries could bridge the gap. Alice's unusual outbursts and temper tantrums did nothing toward bringing her acceptance. Flagler, however, overlooked her faults dismissing them as moodiness. For years the Flaglers lived in a suite in the Ponce de León Hotel as Alice enjoyed her superficial popularity. She hosted numerous balls and loved to exhibit her glamorous wardrobe and jewels. Her extravagance is noted in Sidney Martin's *Florida's Flagler*. She hosted the "Hermitage Ball" in 1893 wearing "a beautiful gown of white tulle, *entraine*, the front bodice being embroidered in mother of pearl and gold and the skirt was bordered with pearl fringe half a yard deep. The bodice was decolleté, the neck being finished with white ostrich. Bows of broad white velvet caught up the short sleeves."

Alice made a point of being the center of attention then, and again a month later when her extravagant pearls were so preposterous *The Tatler* labeled the event the "Pearl Dance."

As Alice's desire to be accepted by the elite led to more and more entertainment, Flagler began construction of a winter home situated beside the Presbyterian Church built in memory of his daughter, Jennie Louise. He named the beautiful but unpretentious Colonial building Kirkside. It was completed in 1893. Alice continued to preside over formal affairs in the hotel ballroom, but more often held intimate gatherings at home.

The year the Flaglers moved into Kirkside began the noticeable decline of Alice's mental faculties. In 1893 she received as a gift the newly invented Ouija board. She became obsessed with it spending hours using the wooden board and planchette to communicate with spirits. Her circle of friends dwindled as she turned to mediums and spiritualists for advice and companionship. As always she spent money excessively in her search for fulfillment. It was not until she became convinced that the Czar of Russia loved her and wanted to marry her that Flagler and his friends became concerned. Her erratic behavior escalated to violence and accusations that Flagler was being unfaithful to her. Always, she repeated she would some day marry the Czar—after her husband's death.

Flagler continued to maintain hope Alice would regain her normalcy and not slip into uncontrollable behavior. Indeed, he loved her despite her faults. In addition to providing her with every luxury she desired, he paid homage to her by bestowing her name on his properties. Alicia Hospital, presented by Flagler to the city of St. Augustine, bore her name from its opening in 1890 until 1905 when it was changed to Flagler Hospital in honor of its benefactor. He again used the name "Alicia," apparently his pet name for her, to designate the private rail car in which they traveled. The luxurious 160-foot yacht seen frequently along Florida's shores and around the waters surrounding the Long Island summer home also bore her name.

The awakening to the depth of Alice's illness can be pinpointed to the occasion of a gathering of family and friends at Lawn Beach. Present was Dr. George G. Shelton, the close family friend who had been with Jennie Louise at her time of death. He had witnessed Alice's outbursts in the past and often tried to deflect her behavior to protect Flagler. This time, however, her actions surpassed anything he had witnessed in the past. After hearing her speak disparagingly not only about Flagler but also other prominent people, he pulled her aside in an attempt to quiet her. His unsuccessful pleas pushed her further into her delusional state. Finally, she produced three stones she claimed had magical powers. She verbally attacked the doctor angrily proclaiming she knew the powers of the stones, but he did not. Holding one up she said, "This one is for the Czar."

Shelton was shocked by her behavior and asked Flagler to meet in his office. He explained his concerns and suggested Alice be moved to the Fifth Avenue home so he could more easily monitor her illness. Flagler agreed and for about a year Alice visited the physician frequently. When her delusions of marrying the Czar of Russia were repeated in public with Alice continually speaking of the marriage as occurring after her husband's death, Shelton began to fear for Flagler's safety. He suggested Flagler not share a bedroom with Alice, but Flagler refused saying his presence had a quieting affect on her. He feared leaving her alone would further exacerbate her delusions.

Shelton finally convinced Flagler to have two of his colleagues interview Alice. On October 24, 1895, Shelton and physicians Allan Starr and Frederick Peterson went to the Fifth Avenue home. Alice was outraged when she learned their intentions and locked herself in her room. The physicians were prepared for resistance and had brought with them papers of commitment. After labeling her condition delusionary insanity, they called in two nurses—one male, one female—who were waiting outside. With Alice screaming for help they placed her in the waiting carriage and took her to Choate's Sanitarium in Pleasantville, New York. Although the asylum was only twenty miles from downtown Manhattan, Flagler never visited his wife there. He was overcome by misery and at Shelton's suggestion left New York for his planned trip to Florida.

While there, Flagler tried to dismiss his concerns by again filling his days with work as he had during his marriage to Mary. He traveled further south in Florida visiting Palm Beach and Miami planning more projects, all the while worrying about his wife. Upon his return in the spring he learned Alice's condition seemed improved. Ignoring warnings of a possible relapse, Flagler happily took Alice back to Lawn Beach in June 1896. Few visitors were allowed at the home except for Elizabeth Adriance Ashley, a cousin of Flagler's on his mother's side. She was one of his favorite relatives and her husband, Eugene Ashley, a New York attorney, shared many business interests with Flagler. The couple planned to stay indefinitely so Elizabeth could provide companionship to Alice.

During the summer Alice's condition worsened and soon after it became necessary to turn Lawn Beach into an asylum with four nurses and a resident doctor caring for Alice. By winter Flagler moved to a hotel in Manhattan and managed a short trip to Florida despite his painful concerns about his wife. During this time Alice became extremely homicidal and despite all precautions managed to hide a pair of scissors and brutally attacked a visiting doctor.

On March 20, 1897, Flagler watched as Alice was forcibly removed from her Lawn Beach house to be recommitted to the Pleasantville asylum. It was the last time he saw her.

In 1899 the courts ruled her incurably insane. Dr. Carlos MacDonald, operator of the asylum, was appointed her medical guardian. Eugene Ashley was named guardian of her property.

Flagler provided well for Ida Alice. She received an income of $120,000 per year from the $1.4 million dollar fund in her name. She had a private cottage and was permitted outings when Dr. MacDonald and nurses could accompany her. Certain of the love of the Czar of Russia, she continued to wait for him maintaining what she believed to be her attractive appearance by giving herself facials with a substance made from coffee cream, applying dye from red yarn to her cheeks, and using burnt cork to accent her eyebrows.

Ida Alice died of a brain hemorrhage July 12, 1930, at the age of eighty-two. She was worth more than fifteen million dollars.

MARY LILY
Mary Lily Kenan Flagler Bingham

In 1901, Florida's divorce law tarnished the reputation of the man who had paved the streets of Florida with gold. After Ida Alice was declared incurably insane in 1899, it was time for Flagler to move on with his life. He had met the woman he wished to wed, but insanity was not grounds for divorce either in his home state of New York or in Florida. Seeing the futility of seeking freedom through New York courts, Flagler looked to Florida. There he had more clout—and he chose to use it. Consulting with his political friends, he managed to convince them of the propriety of enacting a law permitting divorce when the spouse was declared incurably insane.

The Florida divorce law passed April 25, 1901. Flagler's divorce from Ida Alice was granted five months later on August 13. Henry M. Flagler and Mary Lily Kenan were married ten days later on August 24.

Mary Lily and Flagler first met in 1891. Mary Lily was born June 14, 1867, in Wilmington, North Carolina. She was the oldest of the four children of William Rand Kenan Sr. and Mary Hargrave, with siblings Jessie, Sarah, and William Rand Jr. The Kenan family was prominent in the state with a town, "Kenansville," named for them. Mary Lily was raised to be a proper Southern belle and was a graduate of Peace Institute in Raleigh, North Carolina, where she learned social graces and perfected her skills as a pianist and vocalist. After graduation, Mary Lily decided to test the waters of high society and found them to her liking.

Mary Lily's circle of friends included the Pembroke Joneses. Also from the Wilmington area, the Joneses had made their fortune in the cotton and rice industries before retiring to spend winters in St. Augustine and summers in Newport, Rhode Island.

Pembroke Jones also knew Henry Flagler with whom he had mutual interests including railroads, shipping lines, and yachts. In 1891 the Joneses invited Mary Lily, the Flaglers, and the Eugene Ashleys to visit at their Newport home. Although accompanied by his wife, Flagler was taken by the lovely Mary Lily. Ida Alice, too, noticed Mary Lily's charm and was impressed with her style and musical ability. It was not, therefore, unusual when Flagler invited the Joneses, Mary Lily and his favorite cousin Elizabeth Ashley to travel to St. Augustine. He sent a special railroad car for Mary Lily and Elizabeth providing them a luxurious suite at the Ponce de León Hotel with a bevy of maids to pamper them. Mary Lily loved the elegance and the attention she received. Flagler frequently took the young women on outings and trips, a habit that grew as Ida Alice's mental health declined.

Mary Lily was aware of Ida Alice's illness and kept abreast of the situation through contact with Elizabeth. By the time Alice was hospitalized, rumors were rampant. But Flagler and Mary Lily were no strangers to gossip or scandal and were not deterred from their rendezvous. In 1899 Mary Lily's father approached Flagler and asked him his intentions. That was the year Ida Alice was declared insane, but Flagler still did not have the freedom to marry.

On Kenan's mind was the tragedy of his second daughter, Jessie, whose husband, J. Clisby Wise, left her and their infant daughter shortly after Louise Clisby Wise's birth on June 28, 1895.

Flagler had proposed to Mary Lily during a visit in Palm Beach giving her almost one million dollars worth of jewelry including a pearl necklace. However, the Kenan family was not mollified. Finally Flagler reassured Kenan of his sincerity by promising to always take care of Mary Lily, further appeasing him by immediately presenting Mary Lily with a gift of one million dollars worth of Standard Oil stock. Flagler judiciously asked Mary Lily's brother Will, the chief electrical engineer for the Flagler hotel system, to handle the transaction.

With the divorce finalized, in 1901 the wedding ceremony transpired. It was a small affair held at the Kenan family home, Liberty Hall, in Kenansville, North Carolina. Mary Lily's only attendant was her niece Louise who served as flower girl. The couple then honeymooned at the Mamaroneck estate before Flagler went back to business as usual.

As a gift to his bride, he planned a new and beautiful home to her liking in Palm Beach. The Southern-style columnar mansion was completed in 1902 and named Whitehall by Mary Lily. January of that year heralded the first social season in Palm Beach with the new Mrs. Flagler in charge.

Mary Lily was in her element as hostess of some of the grandest functions experienced by the northern visitors who now flocked to sunny Palm Beach. The Flaglers entertained lavishly on holiday occasions with music provided by Russell T. Joy, the organist brought to Whitehall from Memorial Presbyterian Church.

On more intimate occasions the Flaglers enjoyed the company of her family and close friends. Flagler's St. Augustine friend and business confidant Dr. Andrew Anderson visited as did their mutual friends the Ashleys. Mary Lily's parents and siblings came frequently with everyone delighting in the youthful exuberance of Mary Lily's niece Louise, Jessie's daughter.

Flagler had made the transition from St. Augustine smooth by completing the railway south during the decade of the 1890s. By 1890 he reached Daytona, about fifty miles south of St. Augustine. From there he proceeded to New Smyrna, always looking south. By 1893 his rails reached Titusville and by January 1894 the rattling engines steamed all the way to Fort Pierce. All that was left at the time was Palm Beach and work was completed on that section of tracks later in 1894.

During this time Flagler was also keeping busy building the largest wooden hotel in the world, the Royal Poinciana in Palm Beach opening in 1894. His success with the Royal Poinciana was rivaled by his own hotel, The Breakers, which Flagler rebuilt in 1904 after destruction by fire. By this time Flagler and Mary Lily were firmly established in Palm Beach, but Flagler continued looking south. He took his railroad to Miami completing it in April 1896.

Flagler's railroad, by then chartered as Florida East Coast Railroad, now reached from Jacksonville to Miami covering almost the entire length of the state. But Flagler's dream had not reached fruition. He still wanted to take a railroad across the Florida keys to Key West. Despite opposition, he began the project in 1906. It took seven years to complete, but it was a high point in Flagler's life. On January 22, 1912, Mary Lily and Flagler were on the first official train to steam into Key West. The feat was applauded by dignitaries including military person-

Mary Lily Kenan Flagler, Henry Flagler's third wife. (Print from author's collection)

nel, foreign ambassadors, and Florida's Governor Albert Gilchrist. Military music, speeches, and banquets lasted for three days. Flagler was in his glory. It is said he ended one of his speeches saying, "Now I can die happy. My dream has been fulfilled."[2]

Unfortunately, Flagler was aging and his health deteriorating. Mary Lily was always by his side despite any problems, and she was with him at Whitehall on January 15, 1913, when he stumbled and fell on the white marble staircase. His hip was broken and he suffered numerous cuts and bruises. After a few days of rest he appeared to rally but his family and friends knew he would never leave his bed. Business associates were called in and his estranged son Harry, whom he had not seen in many years, came to bid a final farewell. By that time, Flagler was comatose and unable to recognize those around him. His end was near. Mary Lily was one of the few with him when he quietly passed away May 20, 1913.

It was Flagler's wish to be entombed in the mausoleum adjoining Memorial Presbyterian Church in St. Augustine. Flagler had planned the structure in 1901 and upon completion several years later his first wife Mary Harkness Flagler, daughter Jennie Louise, and her baby Margery were all entombed there.

Flagler's body was taken by train from Palm Beach to St. Augustine on May 23 where it lay in state for a few hours in the rotunda of the beautiful Ponce de León Hotel—the hotel that began Flagler's flight into Florida. At three o'clock that afternoon he was taken to Memorial Presbyterian Church where a short service was conducted before the body was placed in the crypt to the right of his wife and daughter. An empty tomb on the opposite side of the mausoleum was intended for Mary Lily. She had agreed to the arrangement in a legal document filed June 20, 1911, in the St. Johns County Court House.[3]

Mary Lily requested no period of mourning be declared in Florida, believing this to be according to the wishes of her late husband. During the early days of her own grieving, Mary Lily accepted an invitation to visit with the Pembroke Joneses in Newport. For months she resided either in their Newport home or with them in New York. She did not return to Whitehall. As time passed she lapsed into despondency and found herself more and more alienated by her friends and family. She had inherited over $100 million in assets from Flagler including cash, Standard Oil holdings, and all the Flagler systems ranging from railroads and hotels to water and electrical companies and newspapers. It all belonged to Mary Lily. She was, in fact, the richest woman in the world.

But she was the richest *widow* in the world and a very lonely one. She let it be known that her wealth would be shared with her family and friends hoping to entice them back. The ploy did not work, however, and she continued her solitary existence spending summers at

Mamaroneck or in a mansion in Asheville, North Carolina.

Her loneliness ended, however, when she was reunited with a former sweetheart from college days, Robert Worth Bingham of Louisville, Kentucky. Bingham's wife had died within weeks of the demise of Flagler, and Bingham and Mary Lily would no doubt have crossed social paths at some juncture. The reunion took place in the summer of 1915 when Bingham was heavily in debt and floundering in his business dealings, social activities, and family life. The attorney known as "the judge" had enjoyed years of political popularity and some social standing through his wife's family, the Longs, pioneers of Louisville, Kentucky. His reputation, both good and bad, had spread beyond Louisville and now he badly needed financial help.

Bingham's young son Barry was being cared for by his sister Sadie Grinnan in Asheville, North Carolina. Mary Lily was staying at a mansion in Asheville. Bingham and Mary Lily met and began seeing each other frequently during the summer of 1915 and again in 1916. By September they decided to marry and the ceremony occurred November 15, much to the chagrin of the Kenan family. Niece Louise Wise, then twenty-one, was present at the wedding as she had been as a child for Mary Lily's nuptials to Flagler.

Mary Lily was happy, but Bingham was not the man she wished him to be. After the honeymoon Mary Lily had been unceremoniously deposited at the Seelbach Hotel in Louisville, an establishment primarily for men with strict rules precluding any social activity. Bingham left early and returned late, sometimes spending days away investing his newly acquired wealth. Women were not allowed in the dining room, so Mary Lily ate her meals in her room. It was a veritable prison for the former social star of the South.

Also, financial arrangements became an issue. Disregarding a prenuptial agreement, Bingham convinced Mary Lily several times to change her will. All the while, Mary Lily was growing sicker. She did find time to search for a rental home and settled on Lincliffe, a twenty-two-acre estate in Louisville in need of repairs. Although the original date set for occupancy was January 1, 1917, progress was far slower than expected. Just prior to Christmas, Mary Lily greeted the three Bingham children with presents and hopes for a happy holiday. The children were sullen and unresponsive. As the weeks in January dragged by with Mary Lily becoming sicker and more disheartened, she decided to open Whitehall for the winter. She and Bingham traveled to Palm Beach in February, but when his children refused to visit for Easter, Mary Lily canceled her parties, closed Whitehall, and the couple returned to Louisville.

By May when the Binghams moved into Lincliffe, Bingham had hired physician and personal friend, Dr. Michael Leo Ratvitch, a dermatologist, to care for Mary Lily. As she tried to settle into life at Lincliffe, Dr. Ratvitch began administering heavy doses of morphine to alleviate her chest pains. The pattern of mistreatment by Dr. Ratvitch and the constant manipulation by Bingham of Mary Lily's will continued over the next few months, alarming family and friends. Her final public appearance was at the Lincliffe housewarming June 9, 1917. Following that she continued to meet with Dr. Ratvitch at his office for daily shots of "medicine." Unable to escape the hot Louisville summer, Mary Lily suffered, becoming weaker. Finally, on July 12, she could stand it no longer and tried to gain relief by soaking in a tub of cold water. When the maid came to check her after an hour, Mary Lily was found slumped over the edge of the tub. She was alive—but barely. Dr. Ratvitch continued to fill her body with morphine, keeping her completely helpless. No heart specialists were brought in. Her brother William and sister Jessie arrived July 26. Mary Lily went into a state of fits the next day and by 3:10 p.m. she died in the throes of hideous convulsions.

Mary Lily was buried in Oakdale Cemetery, the Kenan family plot in Wilmington, North Carolina. The cause of death was listed as heart failure. Rumors later said her own abuse of drugs and alcohol killed her. Soon, however, the rumors shifted to talk of murder—murder by her husband aided by his accomplice Dr. Ratvitch. The evidence was strong enough, and the Kenans persistent enough to warrant further proof of death. Even in death there was no peace for Mary Lily. The controversy resulted in exhuming the body for a final autopsy. No conclusive evidence was found, but her family and friends were convinced her death came at the hands of Robert Worth Bingham.

Although Bingham signed a prenuptial agreement, a codicil signed by Mary Lily dated June 26, 1917, left him $5 million despite Kenan family protests. It was a pittance however to the approximately $150 million estate she left. Of that, $6 million went to each of her sisters and her brother. The largest amount she bequeathed to her beloved niece Louise Clisby Wise who was just twenty-two years of age at the time.

LOUISE
Louise Clisby Wise Lewis Lewis Francis

Louise was not surprised by the enormous inheritance left her by Aunt Mary Lily. Indeed she expected it. Louise loved living the life of a socialite and strove to emulate Mary Lily in the role of quintessential hostess. Louise was, in fact, much like Mary Lily, although tending toward a more flamboyant personality.

Records indicate, Louise Clisby Wise was born in Decatur, Georgia, on June 28, 1895, the daughter of Mary Lily's sister Jessie and J. Clisby Wise. Louise never knew the father who deserted her when she was an infant and she was taken under the wing of her aunts and uncle. Mary Lily, the oldest of the siblings, was unmarried but enjoying the company of Henry Flagler at the time.

When Mary Lily married Flagler in 1901, Louise was there as the six-year-old flower girl and the only attendant. When Whitehall was opened Mary Lily delighted in having young Louise visit. Louise was the only Kenan child of her generation. Of the four siblings, Mary Lily, Jessie, Sarah, and William, only Jessie produced an offspring.

Louise and Jessie continued their visits to the various homes owned by Flagler and apparently he enjoyed Louise's presence immensely. Although stiffly formal in his letter writing, even to his adored Mary Lily, he nonetheless wrote with refreshing affection to Louise. In a letter dated August 2, 1911, when Louise was sixteen he addressed her as "My dear baby" thanking her for her letter to him and affirming he was always happy to hear from her. Along with bits of small talk he assured her that she and her mother were welcome at Mamaroneck anytime and hoped she would come soon. The letter ends, "With dearest love, believe me" and is signed, "Your affectionate Uncle Henry." The relationship was close between aunt and niece and strengthened even more by Flagler's sincere devotion to the fatherless girl.

When Mary Lily was widowed in 1913, seventeen-year-old Louise was by her side and continued as a close companion as Mary Lily battled depression and loneliness in the ensuing years. Louise was the principal heir of Mary Lily's estate and more than happy to accompany her aunt in her travels. Louise was young and beautiful and wanted to share the fairy tale lifestyle of her famous aunt.

When Mary Lily married Robert Worth Bingham in 1916, it was Louise whose sparkle out-shined all others. As bridesmaid she dressed elaborately. A *New York Times* article describes her as being clothed in an ankle-length dress of white broadcloth, adorned with white fox fur. Her white satin hat also was embellished with fur. Mary Lily was dressed subtlety in gray velvet with her million dollar pearl necklace making its own statement.[4]

Mary Lily lived long enough to attend the marriage of her niece. The wedding announcement was made jointly by Mary Lily and her sister, Louise's mother, Jessie Wise. On May 1, 1917, Mary Lily proudly watched as her niece married Lawrence Lewis of Cincinnati, Ohio. Three months later Mary Lily was dead.

At Mary Lily's death Louise was provided with an income of $200,000 a year and a promise of $5 million on her fortieth birthday. In addition she received real estate properties including Lawn Beach at Mamaroneck, Kirkside in St. Augustine, and Whitehall in Palm Beach. Among the jewelry inherited by Louise was the $1 million dollar pearl necklace worn by Mary Lily on her wedding day.

In an odd twist of fate Louise and Lawrence were invited by Bingham to spend some time at Lincliffe, immediately after Mary Lily's death. They were staying in an apartment on the estate and were well cared for by servants. Indeed, it appeared they were given better consideration than Mary Lily ever received at Lincliffe. The plot thickened when, on August 17, the Lewises fled Lincliffe without a note of thanks or an explanation. By the time the press caught up with them they were safely ensconced in the home of Lewis' parents and had called a meeting of the Kenan clan.

Speculation ran from talk of manipulation by Bingham to Kenan family interference in question of the $5 million inheritance expected by Bingham. Friends of Bingham felt he had been badly wronged by the Kenan family, but he finally disappeared from their lives after receiving his entitlement from the June 1917 codicil to Mary Lily's will.

Over the course of time Louise and Lawrence produced two children. Lawrence Lewis Jr. was born July 6, 1918, in Wilmington, North Carolina. Shortly after the birth of their son, Louise moved to St. Augustine where their daughter, Mary Lily Flagler Lewis, called Molly, was born on March 7, 1920. At that time Louise made St. Augustine her principal home at Kirkside, the house originally built for Flagler's second wife Ida Alice. She also spent time in her oceanside cottage, Los Vientos, on St. Augustine Beach.

The Lewis marriage failed, ending in divorce on grounds of desertion in 1926. Shortly after the divorce, Louise married Hugh R. Lewis of Bear Creek, Pennsylvania—no relation to Lawrence.

Hugh was the son of Albert Lewis, a man reputed to be the "Pennsylvania lumber king." In 1900 Albert purchased a large Colonial Revival house on the corner of Cordova and Valencia Streets in St. Augustine. The house was a Henry Flagler construction that the Lewis family named Casa Amarylla. The Lewis children, including Hugh, wintered in the house. In 1918 when Louise moved into Kirkside one block away, the families would certainly have been in close contact and Louise, Lawrence, and Hugh were all in the same age bracket.

After Louise's divorce from Lawrence in 1926, Hugh was comfortably available and he and Louise married, although only for a short time.

Louise's third husband was Frederick G. Francis of St. Augustine whom she married on March 25, 1931. Francis was a sportsman excelling in baseball and was an excellent dancer and singer well liked in town.

Although popular he was, however, a heavy drinker who occasionally exhibited an abusive personality. Socially, he was a good match for Louise who enjoyed an extravagant lifestyle Francis was more than happy to share.

By 1936 Louise purchased the Albert Lewis house, her former father-in-law's home, which remained empty during most of the 1930s. She arranged for remodeling with the intention of converting the home into a charitable preschool she named Flagler Nursery School. The idea was conceived after Louise became associated with a government-operated institution in Baltimore, Maryland. Unfortunately, Louise died before completion of the day care center without endowing it in her will. The building was never used for the thirty-six preschool age children it had been planned to accommodate. Shortly after Louise's death the building was purchased and converted into apartments.

Heiress Louise lived in the fast lane and apparently her $200,000 a year income was not enough to support her in the manner to which she had become accustomed. By 1919 she had sold Lawn Beach, the estate at Mamaroneck, to D.W. Griffith, of silent screen fame. The converted mansion became known as Oriental Point. In 1924 she sold Whitehall to investors who converted the mansion into a luxury hotel, eventually restored as the Flagler Museum.

Louise received the $5 million dollar inheritance on her fortieth birthday as specified in Mary Lily's will. Little time was left for her to enjoy it, however. In May 1937 she was visiting with friends in Short Hills, New Jersey, when she apparently suffered a heart attack and died in Overlook Hospital in nearby Summit. Her son, Lawrence Lewis Jr., eighteen, was at school in Woodberry Forest, Virginia. Daughter Molly, sixteen, was a student at St. Catherine's in Richmond, Virginia. Louise was buried in the family plot at Oakdale Cemetery in Wilmington, North Carolina, the same cemetery in which Mary Lily was interred twenty years before.[5]

As much as Louise loved spending money, she also was a generous philanthropist. Her benevolence was particularly appreciated in St. Augustine. She often aided Memorial Presbyterian Church where Flagler and his family are entombed and where she was a member. In 1926 she financed an addition to the former manse (pastor's house). The addition became known as Fellowship Hall as the building, formerly used as the manse evolved into the Church House for office, Sunday school, and congregational use. The adjacent house, the home of James E. Ingraham, a Flagler official, reverted to the Flagler estate after Ingraham's death in 1924. Louise gave it to the church as a gift to be used as the new home for each Presbyterian minister and his family.

Among her other philanthropic deeds was the attempt to establish Flagler Nursery School for preschool age children from needy families, a project that did not survive her demise.

The *St. Augustine Record* report of her sudden death, published May 30, 1937, noted that, "Mrs. Francis aided many good causes, civic and charitable. She was one of the first to make a generous donation when funds were being raised last fall to show St. Augustine's good faith and its wishes in connection with the coming here of the Carnegie Institution's survey staff to direct the Restoration program.

Her private charities were numerous, and many needy people were the recipients of her beauty. Gifts of this kind were always made quietly, and none will ever know their extent."

A friend who knew Louise well commented for the article, "Mrs. Francis' gifts were always given with such graciousness that she conveyed upon her the idea a favor was being conferred upon her by acceptance. Only a truly warmhearted and unselfish spirit can make gifts in this manner."

The estate of Louise Clisby Wise Lewis Lewis Francis was appraised at $2,177,722.45. Real estate property included Kirkside valued at $44,306; *Los Vientos* at $10,000; and Flagler Nursery School at $12,500. Noted among her personal effects was an expensive pearl necklace.

Of the major properties owned by Louise, only Kirkside was destroyed. In the 1940s it was leased to the University Foundation, a religious school. The following decade when repair and restoration costs amounted to $20,000 Kirkside was demolished rather than saved.

Los Vientos, Louise's place of relaxation, exists on St. Augustine Beach as a bed and breakfast inn overlooking the ocean.

Of all the properties Whitehall in Palm Beach stands as the proud reminder of the Flagler era. It remained a hotel from 1926 until it was purchased in 1959 by Jean Flagler Mathews, one of Harry's three daughters. It opened as a museum the following year and operates today as the Henry Morrison Flagler Museum. To the credit of Mary Lily, for whom it was designed; to Louise, who brightened it with youthful exuberance; and Jean Mathews who saved it, the building now represents an important era in Florida's history—the Golden Age. It is a tribute to the man who gilded the sunshine state and is on the National Register of Historic Places.

THE WIVES

Flagler's mother, sister, and daughters, including young Carrie, profoundly influenced the life of the man who earned his millions through hard work and innovative thinking. But it was his three wives who knew him best.

"Despite Flagler's massive celebrity, he died an unknown man. He had an almost excessive modesty and a personality so elusive as to be unseizable. His sole intimates were his wives; the friend of his boyhood, Dan Harkness; and the friend of his manhood, Andrew Anderson."[6]

CHAPTER VII

Community Contributors

❧

SARAH MATHER and REBECCA PERIT
Educators of the Untutored (1819–1894)

They were simple, straightlaced school teachers . . . or were they? Sarah Mather arrived in St. Augustine in 1857 and successfully opened a private school. Miss Perit joined her in the 1870s. Together the two northern spinsters became an indomitable force in this southern city.

Sarah Ann Mather was born in 1819 in Northampton, Massachusetts. Rebecca Lathrop Perit was a Philadelphia native born in 1824. Both were dedicated schoolteachers and, according to an article in the local society newspaper, *The Tatler*, Miss Perit and Sarah were "life-long friends."[1]

Miss Mather was a graduate of Mount Holyoke Seminary, South Hadley, Massachusetts, one of the first schools in the country to take steps toward the higher education of women. She taught in private schools in Virginia for about fifteen years before leaving for St. Augustine. Her ancestry, education, and concern for people of color and Indians gave her ample fuel for the fire that would burn long and consistently in her tireless efforts toward improving education and introducing Protestant religion to the underprivileged in St. Augustine.

Miss Mather was a descendant of a long line of gospel ministers including the Puritan, Cotton Mather. An undated newspaper obituary in the Bevin Scrapbook, St. Augustine Historical Society, said she began early in life the "education of the untutored of the country." The article also listed her many accomplishments including building a church, organizing a school for the colored people, and assisting in the management of a home for the aged colored.

Rebecca Perit also was involved in humanitarian causes and, according to her *Florida Times-Union* obituary written March 17,

1893, Miss Perit had "inherited a fondness for teaching and in her early life in Massachusetts became imbued with a desire to teach the colored people."[3]

Miss Perit worked diligently beside her friend and branched out to other causes as well. A *Tatler* article notes that "Miss Perit has not been strong for several years past yet her name appears as an active worker in any project for the good of others."[2] She was one of the originators of the Hospital Association of Alicia Hospital in St. Augustine and worked hard to support the health institution. At a benefit for the hospital some of her diamonds, stipulated in her will to aid the institution, were offered for sale. The proceeds were earmarked for funding of a bed known as the Presbyterian bed. The jewels were valued at about $1,365, from which about $300 worth were purchased at the benefit.

Miss Perit was also instrumental in forming the St. Augustine Library Association joining five other prominent residents as a charter member.[3]

Miss Mather was thirty-eight years old when she ventured south; Miss Perit was in her mid- to late forties when she joined her friend who by then was over fifty. As the two strove for educational and religious equality for African Americans, they were presented with a challenge of a different kind. In 1875 more than seventy Native Americans arrived by train from the Great Plains states to be imprisoned for what resulted in a three-year term at Fort Marion (now the Castillo de San Marcos).

The two women were likely among those residents curiously watching as seventy-some shackled and dirty Indian prisoners traipsed slowly across the drawbridge and into the old fort.

Exiled from their home in the western Plains, the Indians were tired and sick after the long journey and presented a pitiful rather than frightening sight. As the soldiers busied themselves with the task of healing the infirm and arranging for as much comfort as possible in the old fort, Miss Mather elected to provide for their education. Her work, in fact, was recognized in a sketch in *Harper's Bazaar* magazine of May 11, 1878. Two other St. Augustine residents, Julia (Mrs. George Couper) Gibbs and Laura (Mrs. Kingsley) Gibbs, are also mentioned. Winter visitor Amelia (Mrs. Horace) Caruthers devoted her time in the classroom during her stay in town and Anna Pratt, the wife of Captain Richard Pratt who was in charge of the Indians, also were depicted.

Miss Perit is not mentioned in the magazine write-up but does appear in *Battlefield and Classroom*, a book by Captain Richard Pratt, the supervisor of the Indians during the three-year confinement.

Pratt describes the work of the women noting they were excellent ladies who "volunteered to give daily instruction to the prisoners in classes, and throughout their whole prison life there were from four to six classes almost constantly under instruction."

As the years wore on, Captain Pratt struggled to place the brighter young Indians in homes and schools in northern United States cities. Pratt wrote of his efforts and the antics of Miss Mather in his book. The first concern was money and the ladies of the town, certainly with the persuasion and help of Miss Mather and Miss Perit, decided to orchestrate an entertaining production as a fundraiser.

They used their own children—eight years of age or younger—to produce a version of *Mother Goose*. The Indian men were persuaded to participate in the program with an Indian dance, War Whoop, love song, and demonstration of Indian sign language.

The program (which cost one dollar, an expensive benefit in those days) was a huge success and was influential in persuading several families to finance the schooling of some of the Indians in their late teens or early twenties.

Each family sponsored one to four children until the number reached almost twenty. It was then Pratt's responsibility to locate the appropriate educational facilities for the young men.

Again, Miss Mather stepped in, writing to General Samuel Chapman Armstrong of the Hampton (Virginia) Agricultural School for Negroes. The two friends shared a mutual interest in educating Negroes. Armstrong was persuaded at first to take one child, but after correspondence, agreed to educate seventeen of the young Indians.

This done, Pratt and his wife left for Carlisle, Pennsylvania, where he was told to proceed to the Indian territory to secure a total of 120 boys and girls to be brought East to be educated.

Pratt immediately wired Miss Mather requesting she join him in this venture. Miss Mather, at age sixty-three, eagerly agreed to join Pratt in Carlisle. They traveled west by train and riverboat with a destination of Rosebud Agency, a governmental settlement west of the Missouri River and just north of the Kansas border.

The last one hundred miles of the trip was spent in a two-seated springboard wagon with only four blankets the Indian driver had brought for himself. When it was necessary to stop for the night, a bed was made for Miss Mather in the back of the wagon using two of the blankets. Pratt and the driver slept under the wagon, each covered by one of the two remaining blankets.

The bitter cold forced them to travel early the next morning and

Sarah Mather and Rebecca Perit were two of the women of the town who learned Indian bow and arrow techniques in exchange for teaching reading and writing. (From Harper's Bazaar *Magazine. Photographic print in author's collection)*

the hardships of the trip included Miss Mather's illness. During the second day, Pratt said Miss Mather became "wretchedly seasick" and the driver was forced to stop several times. Upon reaching the agency a "very capable agency physician soon restored her equilibrium."

Pratt and Miss Mather together convinced the Indian chiefs to send their children back with them so they could "acquire the same education and industries as our white youth had . . ." and, Pratt argued convincingly, education would "make them equals of our youth." The Indian chiefs agreed and Pratt departed for Pine Ridge Agency, further west, leaving Miss Mather alone with the agents and Indians as he gathered more children for the cause.

Although Pratt was well aware of the government's philosophy about taking the children East, it is doubtful that Miss Mather ever realized that humanitarian causes had little to do with the displacement of the children. They were literally taken as hostages to ensure peace among the warring tribes of the Plains.

Miss Mather returned to St. Augustine to find that, in 1886, she once again would be teaching Indians from the West. Five hundred Chiricahua Apaches crowded into Fort Marion and Miss Mather along with Miss Perit and several other townswomen found themselves providing daily class work to the Indians during their year's stay at the fort.

Miss Mather's humor and spunk is personified in two stories describing incidents where she extracted her false teeth in front of her students to their shock and delight.

Pratt writes that author Harriet Beecher Stowe, a winter resident of Florida and a friend of Miss Mather, was observing a class one day when Pratt heard "quite a commotion." The women, he said, "were laughing heartily," but apparently the Indians were dumbstruck. One had his hands in front of his eyes and said "Miss Mather no good."

Pratt discovered that Miss Mather had removed her teeth while trying to instruct her pupils in the correct pronunciation of "th" as in "teeth." Mrs. Stowe went on to further describe the Indian school in several New York publications.

The second incident of Miss Mather's uninhibited behavior took place among the Apache prisoners. It is said she had little difficulty in maintaining discipline. "One day when the students were a bit unruly, she pulled her false teeth out of her mouth; so awed were the Indians that respectful quiet ensued at once."

Despite the unusual circumstances leading the women to work with Native Americans, they always pursued the quest to provide education and religion to the African Americans. Miss Mather was an outspoken critic of slavery and occasionally irritated the southerners of St. Augustine. However, she tread carefully concealing her Northern views while entertaining Confederate troops. An anonymous writer to the *St. Augustine Evening News*, on January 1, 1895, accused the late Miss Mather of hiding her true loyalties through her outward gestures of friendship to the Confederacy. Thomas Graham in *The Awakening of St. Augustine* points out the letter reflects the bitterness still lingering decades after the war. A prominent citizen, Dr. Andrew Anderson defended her in a letter to the editor of the *Evening News* saying her views were always clear and she was "a women of strong character. Her opinions on every subject were decided and well known to her associates. . . ." Anderson's mother was a Northern supporter so it was not unusual for the anonymous letter to elicit such a response from him. Miss Mather did, however, have much to contend with as a Northerner in a southern town.

Miss Perit had not yet arrived in St. Augustine at the time of the Civil War, but was probably doing her share toward the Northern cause while still teaching in Massachusetts. After her arrival in St. Augustine in the 1870s, the two followed the quest they loved best, the education of the colored people.

The first tangible example of their work was the construction sometime prior to 1885 of a modest wooden church on a westside lot on Granada Street. The 1885 bird's-eye view sketch of St. Augustine lists the chapel only as the "Colored Presbyterian Church." Ten years later it was given the name Mather-Perit Church in honor of the two amazing women from the North.

The Mather-Perit Church is listed in the 1895 General Assembly Minutes with a membership of fifteen. Three supply ministers led the flock from 1895–1907. In late 1907 or early 1908 the Reverend James Henry Cooper arrived and guided the congregation until his death in 1938.

A *St. Augustine Record* article in 1908 noted that the lot on which the Mather-Perit Church stood was purchased and the building moved to a lot on the corner of Park Place and Washington Street.

In addition to ministering to the members, Reverend Cooper established a Presbyterian Parochial and Industrial School, often called the Mather-Perit School. Both the school and the church are listed in the 1911–1912 City Directory. Miss Mather was president of the Ladies Executive Board of the school that was quite successful, growing from 106 students in 1916 to 156 in 1923.

The school apparently closed after Reverend Cooper's death as a *St. Augustine Record* article in August 1940 reports that the rambling two-story building then known as Cooper's Hall was to be removed to clear the lot for a playground.

The Reverend Franklin P. Diggs became the church leader in the 1940s, but a fire destroyed the building in 1942 leaving the small congregation without a church home.

In the 1980s two sisters, Petronilla "Pet" Clark and Vondalyn "Von" Clark, who were members of the Mather-Perit Church, related that their grandparents, Brook and George W. Chavas, were active in the church as were their parents, Pearl and Theodore "Red" Clark. Their father was instrumental in initiating a building project in the 1950s but it was not begun until two years after his death in 1962. Today, the walls of the unfinished building still stand on a lot at 106 Washington, now the property of the St. Augustine Presbytery. Until recently the teachers' names appeared on a sign in front of the concrete block walls of the unfinished structure; thus perpetuating the Mather-Perit association with the congregation although no formal church existed.

Work with the home for the aged and indigent colored endowed by humanitarian Buckingham Smith was also included in Miss Mather and Miss Perit's ministry. In a *Tatler* article dated February 18, 1893, mention is made that, "The home for indigent and aged colored people, endowed by Buckingham Smith, has been managed by Miss Perit and Miss Mather of late years as an industrial school for colored children." Miss Mather is also listed in the Chapin Directory of 1885 and other nineteenth century city directories as the Secretary of the Colored Industrial School, President of the Ladies Executive Board of the Colored Industrial School, and on the Board of Lady Managers for the Buckingham Smith Benevolent Society.

Both Miss Mather and Miss Perit left their mark on this city, though they were Northern ladies who probably never knew what tasks were before them here in the "lazy" South. That they were successful is obvious in the esteem placed on them by writers such as Pratt and by the African American's desire to name the church and school for them.

Miss Perit died in 1893 at age sixty-nine survived briefly by her lifelong friend Miss Mather who died March 1894 at age seventy-four. A service for Miss Perit was held at the home the friends shared on King Street. She was lauded in a *Florida Times-Union* article of March 17, 1893, as "one of the two most indefatigable benefactors of the colored people of St. Augustine." After the service, her body was accompanied to the gravesite "followed by people who loved and honored the life of their departed friend."

The funeral for Miss Mather the following year also began with a service at the King Street home after which her body was taken to Memorial Presbyterian Church. Her funeral notice mentioned that the casket was followed by "numerous friends, Sunday School and children of the colored home and many other colored people." Four colored men carried the coffin with honorary pall bearers nearby.

Both women were loved by the community and their names live on in the history of African Americans and Native Americans of the nineteenth century. Tour guides at the fort where the Indians were imprisoned often explain about the women who gave their time toward teaching those held captive. Members of Memorial Presbyterian Church where both women worshiped often related their story. Educators in the community today are aware of the contributions made by Sarah Ann Mather and Rebecca Lathrop Perit toward the schooling of the "untutored"—the African Americans and Native Americans of the nineteenth century. Their work will not be forgotten.

☙

HENRIETTA WHITEMAN
The Indian Side of the Story (1990)

Sarah Mather and Rebecca Perit believed in their hearts educating the Native American prisoners at Fort Marion was a noble service they provided for the "unfortunate savages." Richard Henry Pratt, an officer in the United States Army, believed taking Indian children from their homes to be educated in boarding schools was a benign and tactically effective method of shaping the Native Americans in the white man's ways.

Henrietta Whiteman, great-granddaughter of one of the seventy-two prisoners from the Western Plains, believes they were wrong. Her great-grandmother, White Buffalo Woman, survived the massacre at Sand Creek in 1864; she was encamped near the Washita River in 1868 when the Seventh Calvary under the command of George Armstrong Custer attacked; and she watched the military men shackle her husband and seventy-one other Indians to be transported to Florida.

Ms. Whiteman knew all these stories before she visited St. Augustine's Castillo de San Marcos (the former Fort Marion) in 1991. The experience was highly emotional as she walked the terreplein where her ancestors stood in 1875 gazing for the first time at the immense body of water called the Atlantic Ocean. She toured the dark, damp rooms that circled the courtyard where her people sometimes danced to entertain the tourists and townspeople.

Although much of what the American military did was in good faith or perhaps ignorance, not hostility, the fact remains that a generation of Native Americans was effectively weakened in numbers and in spirit. In addition to teaching them to read, write, and speak English, the military strove to change their outward appearance as well. Indian clothes were replaced with military uniforms. The most atrocious blow of all came when the soldiers cut off the long, dark locks of the red men. Ms. Whiteman said, "It must have been horrifying because to us, cutting one's hair is a sign of mourning—or death."

After three years of imprisonment the men were returned to the West to land designated as reservation sites for each of the tribes. The United States government was steadfastly trying to cultivate the Indians—or kill them. As various methods for reducing the Indian problems were discussed, Pratt came up with what he considered a well-thought-through plan of educating the Indian children. With support from

Henrietta Whiteman poses on the terreplein of the Castillo de San Marcos. (Photo by Karen Harvey, used courtesy of Nebraska ETV)

Washington, D.C., he began the establishment of the first Indian school. In September 1879 he and Miss Mather gathered children from the Western Plains and took them from their homes. Carlisle Indian School in Pennsylvania was the first of several industrial schools for Native Americans eventually mushrooming across thirteen states. However, the grand experiment was a failure with many children dying and others simply tolerating the treatment until they could return home. Only a few remained in the Americanized world. Most were never heard from again.

The ladies of St. Augustine and Pratt were well-meaning Americans who innocently wronged the Indians and cannot be rebuked. Others ridiculed and demeaned the Native Americans with slogans like, "The only good Indian is a dead Indian," "The Swine will return to his wallow, the savage to his barbarism," or "You can no more civilize an Apache than you can civilize a rattlesnake!" They are the ones who pushed the Indians beyond their tolerance.

The teachers believed they were saving souls—never suspecting that the children had values of their own. Henrietta Whiteman ends the poignant video, *In the White Man's Image*, speaking for all her people. "I have not for one second given up what it means for me to be a Cheyenne person. The Cheyenne spirit is enduring."

※

THE ANDERSON FACTOR
Three Generations in a Developing City (1832–1990)

The Anderson women reflect a gentility and grace extending over a century and a half from 1839 to 1990. Their stories encompass not only their own contributions as women in St. Augustine, but those of their contemporaries as well.

The first Anderson woman of mention was Clarissa Cochran Fairbanks, a woman who proved her courage by marrying the widow of her friend and remaining in territorial Florida after his death building his dream.

Mary Anderson's dying wish was that her husband would marry her best friend. It worked out exactly as Mary wanted, but not as new wife Clarissa Cochran Fairbanks expected.

Dr. Andrew Anderson, his wife Mary, and daughters Hannah and Emily arrived from the civilized North to the marshy shores of St. Augustine in December 1829. Mary's health was fragile but her spirit indomitable and she eagerly watched her husband wander from his medical duties to experiments in land ventures.

Daughter Mary was born within a year of the family's arrival and Dr. Anderson continued with plans to develop orange groves, harvest mulberry trees, and cultivate the land west of the town proper. It was in 1832 during the earliest years of territorial growth that Mary's friend Clarissa visited. A New Hampshire native and recently widowed, she ventured forth in 1832 to visit her friend in the steamy South. She traveled by four-wheel carriage from Norfolk, Virginia, and stayed at the boarding house of Mrs. Eliza Whitehurst, the establishment on Aviles Street now known as the Ximénez-Fatio House.[1]

During the visit, Clarissa explored the land, listened to Dr. Anderson's dreams, and spent time not only with Mary and Andrew, but also with the young Anderson girls, including toddler Mary. She returned north but kept in touch as over the years Anderson continued to expand his real estate holdings and orange grove ventures.

Between 1833 and 1838 Anderson purchased plots of land ultimately covering a twenty-acre area. The boundaries equate to current King and Valencia Streets to the south and north, respectively, with Cordova Street to the east and the San Sebastian River running its course along the western banks.

Recovering from the freeze of 1835 that destroyed his orange crop, the ever optimistic doctor embarked on a new project of mulberry tree cultivation for transport to the North with his brother Smith as his agent, as had been the situation with the sale of oranges. Unfortunately this was also the time of simmering Seminole tensions resulting in the well-founded fear of Indian attack. Anderson considered the prospect of selling his property and reestablishing the family in a more secure atmosphere but, on the other hand, he also was looking toward his future in Florida.

Mary's health was deteriorating as she summoned her friend to come and care for the children and the prospective new house planned in the southeast acreage. Mary died before her friend could answer but Clarissa immediately responded to a second plea by Dr. Anderson to come and help him after Mary died in September 1837.

Clarissa was thirty-seven years of age, by some standards old for starting a new life, but nonetheless young enough to take over the household responsibilities as Dr. Anderson's wife. The two were married March 27, 1838. Baby Andrew, always referred to as the second Andrew Anderson, was born March 13 the following year.

At this point life was rosy enough for Dr. Anderson to pursue his plans for a grand manor on his plantation west of the city proper. The acreage had been called Markland since 1834 and all that was needed was to build a residence on the extensive property. Coquina blocks hewn from indigenous stone were brought in and the cornerstone laid in October 1839. Unfortunately, the increasing excitement of new home construction quickly dissipated. Yellow fever crept though the city snatching the lives of the weakened inhabitants. Of those severely struck by the epidemic was Dr. Andrew Anderson who died from the dreaded disease on November 7, 1839.

Mary Elizabeth "Bessie" Anderson. (Photo courtesy Clarissa Anderson Gibbs)

Clarissa was now twice widowed and alone with a baby living in primitive conditions far away from her native New Hampshire and her family. The older Anderson girls, Hannah and Emily, had long since returned to school and relatives in the North. Young Mary likely followed shortly after Anderson's death. As Clarissa recovered from the sting of death it seemed probable she would return to friends and family in her native New Hampshire or her husband's relatives in the state of New

York. But Clarissa chose to live her husband's dream and complete the house on the acreage called Markland.

In Thomas Graham's *The Awakening of St. Augustine,* he says this about Clarissa Cochran Fairbanks Anderson:

> *Mrs. Anderson's relatives could not understand her willingness to remain in St. Augustine, amid a population of half-foreign people, where murderous Indians still burned and looted almost within sight of her home. They advised her to come North where she would not be deprived of the comfort of her religion and the stimulation of intellectual pursuits. But she was captivated by Florida and had no desire to escape its thralls.* [2]

Her letters to friends were similar to those Floridians write today gloating about opening windows to the cool breezes while those up north shiver in the snow. In one letter she marveled at her busy life of entertaining visitors as she also watched over the animals, the grove, and the gardens. She didn't complain—she simply commented on a busy and fulfilling life. Despite the heat and untamed land she saw beauty in the city.

When she was able to resume construction on Markland, she reduced plans by almost half. However, she managed to keep it spacious enough to handle borders during the winter months. Although Clarissa did arrange summer visits to the North, Markland was her home and St. Augustine her town. It was in that house in St. Augustine where her son was raised and where his love and understanding of the town matured.

Another widow holding her own along with Clarissa Anderson was Sarah Peck. Sarah Peck's husband, Dr. Seth Peck, died in July 1841, just two years after the death of Dr. Andrew Anderson. When the coccus attack of destructive insects infected her trees, Clarissa turned to Sarah for financial assistance. Clarissa was determined to make Markland a successful venture and Sarah willingly obliged.

While Clarissa struggled to keep her plantation productive, another issue affected all women in the community. For Florida to gain admittance into the union it was necessary to have a population of 45,000 free, white, male property holders. Clarissa Anderson and Sarah Peck qualified on all counts except "male."

A *Florida Herald and Southern Democrat* editorial of February 20, 1840, warned that women should not be concerned with regulations belonging to men. They should, it said, be involved with household matters, not political issues. Sarah Peck's daughter Rebecca, in her mid-twenties, called the local political situation "laughable, absurd and ridiculous."[3]

After statehood was established in 1845 women, although land-holders, still could not vote as they were in the "unfortunate position" of being female.

During the years of Florida's growth as a state of the Union, Clarissa remained active maintaining her plantation and raising young Andrew who rebelled at leaving St. Augustine for boarding school, but later became a productive student at Princeton University. It was during his Princeton years that Andrew's young love, Helen Porter Baldwin, died of typhoid in St. Augustine in 1859. He corresponded regularly with "Nellie" before her death and was devastated by the loss. It was years before he considered another emotional commitment to a woman.

Clarissa, Northern by birth and temperament, disapproved of Florida's secession from the Union but remained in St. Augustine during the Civil War years. Andrew, at age twenty, chose neutrality (or Clarissa chose for him) by staying up North as a student at the College of Physicians and Surgeons in New York City.

Clarissa spent the war years remaining cordial to her female friends of Southern persuasion including Frances Kirby Smith, mother of Confederate General Edmund Kirby-Smith, and Anna Dummett who expressed her disapproval by chopping down the plaza flagpole upon which was raised the Union colors during Northern occupancy. Also among her friends was Mrs. George Couper Gibbs who proudly fashioned the national flag of Florida that was raised above the town square amidst cheers and artillery salutes shortly after secession was announced.[4]

Fortunately for Mrs. Anderson, not all the women of the town were Southern sympathizers. Union occupancy formally occurred in March 1862 calming Mrs. Anderson and others with ties to Northern states. Retired New England school teachers Miss Sarah Mather and Rebecca Perit also remained true to the Union cause. It was Sarah who joyfully informed Clarissa of the second attempt early in 1863 to rid the city of disloyal families who were considered disruptive.[5]

Clarissa was equably maintaining her role as mistress of Markland when Andrew managed a short visit in 1863 before returning to New York to continue medical studies. As the outcome of the war approached Clarissa kept her homestead functioning beyond expectations. Her watchful, hands-on approach to management resulted in a substantial orange grove to provide a comfortable income for her household staff and maintain the plantation. The orchards and watermelon sales produced hundreds of dollars in profits and was supplemented with income from boarders at Markland. She was not in any way desperate or destitute.

Although she occasionally complained to her son that she needed "an efficient man," she was highly complimented by Andrew when he wrote, "what an enterprising proprietress that place has. . . . No doubt it will be the finest place in all Florida." For a woman alone during a war, Clarissa held her own.[6]

By the mid-1860s Andrew Anderson was back in town and filling his role as physician, churchman, city official, and the town's most eligible bachelor.

The most dramatic event during the 1870s was the arrival of seventy-four Native Americans captured from five tribes in the Plains states for imprisonment at Fort Marion (the Castillo de San Marcos) from 1875 to 1878. Clarissa was unable physically to participate in their welfare, but her younger friends Sarah Mather, Rebecca Perit, and the "Gibbs sisters"—Laura Smethurst Gibbs and Julia Smethurst Gibbs—participated regularly in the education of the men during their three-year incarceration.

In 1879 Clarissa was saddened to learn of the death of her friend Sarah Peck who died at the age of eighty-eight. Sarah left daughters Rebecca and Mary in charge of the large house on the corner of St. George and Treasury Streets, a building old in comparison to Clarissa's Markland, but equally significant in the life of the community.

Clarissa's own health was failing daily and in 1881 she died in the home she had loved and lived in for forty years. Ownership and care of Markland then passed to her son Andrew who found loneliness a difficult burden to bear. For the next decade and a half he rented out rooms in Markland and lived as a tenant outside his childhood home.

In the 1880s the seams burst in the St. Augustine community when Henry Morrison Flagler arrived and plunked his major moneymaking hotel right down beside Markland. Dr. Andrew Anderson, as a native son and prominent citizen, became Flagler's foremost St. Augustine liaison as Flagler's hotels, churches, and community buildings propelled the Spanish settlement into the Gilded Age.

For Dr. Anderson, it spelled more than prosperity—it brought him a wife. Mary Gibbs Smethurst Tyler Grant, a relative of the woman who entered Anderson's life, explained the situation. Grant's English-born grandfather, the father of Anderson's soon-to-be bride, was one of those enticed by the splendor of St. Augustine touted as "The Newport of the South." William Arthur Smethurst had migrated to Philadelphia where he and his first wife Emeline Miller became parents of Mary Elizabeth "Bessie" born in 1864. After Emeline's death Smethurst married Mary

*Clarissa Anderson Gibbs celebrated her ninetieth birthday at
Markland in 1985. She cheerfully modeled a dress from her mother's
time period.*

Williams Gibbs and both continued the care and upbringing of young
Bessie. How and when William Arthur Smethurst met Mary Williams
Gibbs is uncertain, although it is known she did attend school in the
North when war was declared and they could have crossed paths then.[7]

Mary was born in 1844 on Fort George Island near Fernandina,
Florida, and became the Florida connection. She was the daughter of
Kingsley Beatty Gibbs who had inherited the island from his uncle
Zephaniah Kingsley, a prominent landowner of the early 1800s.

Mary and the Gibbs family fled the ravages of the Civil War

forcing them from the St. Augustine home at 20 Bay Street and from the Fort George Island plantation. Mary's father died in 1859 as war approached. Northern friends of the Gibbs family helped them find safety outside of Florida and it is possible that Mary met her future husband Arthur during this time. They were married in 1870 and lived much of the time in Philadelphia where Bessie's half-sister Alice was born on July 31, 1881.

Mrs. Grant who speaks for the family is the daughter of Alice and niece of Bessie. She recalls family lore that as the town of St. Augustine blossomed, the Smethurst family became frequent visitors to the playground for the wealthy. She said, "After his (William Arthur's) first wife died he went to Florida where he met my grandmother, Mary Williams Gibbs." This would have been a pre-Flagler era and whether they met in Florida or in the North is conjecture at this point. They nonetheless divided their time between Philadelphia and Florida.

As Mrs. Grant continued to discuss her grandfather she said he had come to love the blossoming town of St. Augustine. "At that time St. Augustine was a very popular place to go for Northerners. Flagler came to St. Augustine and opened up the Ponce de León Hotel," she related. Indeed Flagler did open the Ponce de León in 1888 and at some time during those golden days, Dr. Andrew Anderson and Mary Elizabeth "Bessie" Smethurst formed a relationship. One can assume that both her father's intrigue with the town and her stepmother's blue-blooded Florida connections gave Bessie a feeling of home and familiarity in St. Augustine. As she grew older she became embroiled in St. Augustine's social whirl which included associating with the town's most notable bachelor.

The glorious day of their marriage occurred January 29, 1895. The groom was fifty-five, the bride thirty-one. The ceremony conducted in Trinity Episcopal Church included Mr. and Mrs. Henry (Ida Alice) Flagler among the many well wishers. It was the last public appearance before Ida Alice's deteriorating mental condition resulted in her confinement.

Graham commented about "Bessie" in *The Awakening of St. Augustine,* noting she was, "A charming woman with considerable strength of will, twenty-four years his junior, whom Anderson had known since her childhood."[8] This indicates the Smethurst family had been part of St. Augustine's society for a long time and the Anderson women were increasingly woven into the fabric of the community. Two other Smethurst sisters intertwined in St. Augustine's society were daughters of William Arthur and Mary Gibbs Smethurst and half-sisters to Bessie.

One sister, Alice, married the Reverend Samuel Tyler in 1911 with the reception held at Markland under the supervision of sister Bessie. A second sister, Mary, named after her mother, figured prominently in the Anderson family as Bessie's health weakened over the years.

From the day of her wedding, Bessie stepped into the role vacated by the first Mrs. Anderson, but under extremely different circumstances. Her position not only involved responsibilities associated with the Anderson name and the Markland home, but also reached out into a far bigger community than St. Augustine had been in Clarissa Anderson's day.

First there was the issue of Markland. Although sitting in the shadows of Flagler's hotels, Markland remained a symbol of Southern living with its inviting verandas and pleasant gardens. Anderson had avoided living in his childhood home after the death of his mother, but eagerly returned to the familiar rooms with his new wife. Of utmost priority to the newlyweds whose ages bore consideration, was bringing children into the world. The births came quickly with Clarissa, named for her grandmother, born November 6, 1895, and the third Andrew Anderson making his appearance on December 8 one year later.

With this new lease on life, Andrew decided to follow his father's dream and enlarge the house to the standards once envisioned by the senior Anderson. Expansion began in the spring of 1899 as Bessie, the children, and Dr. Anderson watched from comfortable quarters in a nearby cottage. With the house doubled in size, luxury, and efficiency, Markland became a center for social activity.

Bessie Anderson was in a new home with a new family and in an unusual position. She was on the fringes of the ultrawealthy, yet she needed to maintain the family traditions and principals that would keep her afloat in small-town St. Augustine. Her choices were few. The sun had not yet risen on the day when women could seek careers of their own no matter how competent or talented they might be. Coping with the lifestyle of the times, Bessie and her compatriots found their days spent either at social events or charity work, often mixing the two in a blend of humanitarian generosity with a flair for entertainment.

Some traditions had already been established regarding the appropriate work projects for gentlewomen. One such charitable group was initiated when Dr. Anderson became involved in the formation of the Flagler-sponsored hospital named Alicia Hospital for Ida Alice. The legend is that Flagler called the women of the town to the rotunda of the Ponce de León Hotel on March 22, 1888, offering a challenge to finance a health facility if the women would form an organization to maintain it. It is not impossible to imagine Bessie, twenty-four years old at the time, accepting such a challenge.

The women immediately went about soliciting contributions and organizing fundraising events including annual charity fairs and George Washington Birthday Balls. The name of Alicia Hospital was changed to Flagler Hospital in 1905 and the Hospital Auxiliary, formed in 1888, continued under the new name. Today the Auxiliary is comprised of both men and women active in the hospital with members staffing the information desks, running the gift shop, delivering patient mail, and assisting with administration and discharge duties.

Bessie's influence in support of the irreplaceable organization was obvious in 1897 when Markland's lawn was the setting for a lavish garden party to benefit Alicia Hospital. Her name appears on the list of Auxiliary members as does her daughter's name in later years and that of Miss Mary Smethurst (Bessie's half sister) who was president of the organization in 1917.

Charitable groups were the backbone of the work of the women of status in the town. The impressive Woman's Exchange, extremely active today, was founded in the late nineteenth century as an outgrowth of the King's Daughters. Both groups gave women an opportunity to put their business acumen to work. King's Daughters' projects for the sick and poor extended to helping women help themselves through an "Industrial Exchange." The purpose was to market the goods made by women from their own homes. By 1893 the Exchange, later called The Woman's Exchange, became fully operational with Anna Gardner Burt its treasurer. Today the Woman's Exchange operates from the Peña-Peck House, the home of Seth and Sarah Peck and later the residence inherited by Anna Burt. The shop of homemade goods and related items is open to the public in the antebellum museum home. The last of the Smethurst sisters, Mary, was president of the Exchange during the 1930s before her death in 1937.

The charity work of Mrs. Anderson may well have been a welcome relief compared to the social obligations. During the winter seasons women of status held an "at home" afternoon during which female guests would drop by and mingle over tea and cookies during the prescribed hours. Events including male guests also were held on a regular basis in Markland as well as other homes of the town's upper-level families.

In 1904 a large gathering was held at Markland to which young Clarissa, age nine, participated. *The Tatler* reported "Mrs. Anderson received her guests with her little daughter Clarissa, receiving with her wearing a dainty white dress." The orchestra from the Alcazar Hotel played for the event attended by the military governor of Cuba as well as other dignitaries.[9]

Graham noted that Mrs. Anderson "lived an active life, not only as a hostess, but also as a contributor of her time to charitable work. When family dinner talk did not center on Dr. Anderson's labors for Alicia Hospital and the Presbyterian Church, it concerned Mrs. Anderson's work as president of Woman's Exchange, a position she held for 12 years."

Mary Elizabeth "Bessie" Anderson accomplished much during her short life. She died September 12, 1912, at the age of forty-eight.

The third of the Anderson women, named Clarissa for her grandmother, was not yet seventeen when her mother died. With the welfare of younger brother Andrew also of consideration, Dr. Anderson sought the help of Bessie's half sister Mary Smethurst. "Aunt Mary" came to live at Markland to run the house and be a companion to Clarissa. The two frequently spent time in Nova Scotia together.

Although Clarissa grew up in Markland, her school years were spent away at St. Timothy's, a boarding school outside Baltimore, Maryland. After her mother's death she returned to Markland to be with her father. Her interests in St. Augustine kept her busy. Mrs. Grant noted that although Clarissa did not receive further formal education, "she was an extremely well-informed person, always interested in St. Augustine." She said Clarissa followed in her father's footsteps in that regard.

In 1929 Markland was the scene of her wedding to John Dimick and her life took her away from St. Augustine. The two traveled extensively including living in Guatemala where Clarissa's interest in archeology was stimulated. The couple adopted a son, John Cochran Dimick; however, Clarissa and John divorced in 1939.

It has been said that the great love of Clarissa's life was Tucker Carrington Gibbs, with whom she grew up in St. Augustine.[10] Both went their separate ways in early adulthood. Clarissa married and spent time away traveling. Tucker also married and joined the Navy serving in both World War I and II. After retirement Gibbs, then single, returned to St. Augustine where he was reunited with the divorced Clarissa whom he married.

Clarissa's love for Tucker and allegiance to the Gibbs family through her mother is evident in the naming of the building she gave to Flagler Hospital. The Anderson-Gibbs Building was constructed in 1989 as an office building with a pharmacy adjoining the hospital. The three-story structure was dedicated to the memory of Clarissa's father, Dr. Andrew Anderson, and her late husband, Tucker C. Gibbs, who had served as a member of the Board of Trustees of Flagler Hospital. When the new

Flagler Hospital was constructed in 1989, an addition for doctors' offices was again named the Anderson-Gibbs Building. The dedication plaque states it was "Named for three of Flagler Hospital's principal benefactors; Dr. Andrew Anderson, 1839–1924, Pioneer Flagler Hospital Physician and Philanthropist; His Daughter Clarissa Anderson Gibbs 1895– ; and Her Husband Tucker Carrington Gibbs, 1889–1965."

Clarissa Anderson Gibbs also honored the church of her father and grandfather, Memorial Presbyterian Church in St. Augustine. Her grandfather had been elected a trustee of Memorial's predecessor, St. Augustine's First Presbyterian Church. Her father had served the longest time period as an officer in Memorial Presbyterian Church working in the capacity of elder and trustee for fifty-nine years.

Mrs. Gibbs presented two valuable gifts to the church in 1978. One was a painting of St. Augustine executed in the 1600s by Francisco de Herrera, a native of Sevilla, Spain. The second gift was a copy of *The City of God*, Saint Augustine's treatise written in Latin and published in 1475. The painting and book were inherited by Mrs. Gibbs from the Peck family and passed on to the church in memory of both families.

In 1990 Mrs. Gibbs died at age ninety-four in St. Augustine.

The Anderson women spanned three separate eras: Territorial, the Gilded Age, and Modern Times. All three were products of their environment. Clarissa Cochran Fairbanks was unfailingly faithful to her husband's dream while living in a primitive town. She got her hands dirty in the orange groves but put on the white gloves to serve tea to Union soldiers. She maintained a house and a plantation and sent a son to medical school.

Mary Elizabeth "Bessie" Smethurst successfully navigated the waters of the wealthy and left her mark of good works on society. She taught her daughter polished manners and a sense of responsibility to her community.

Clarissa Anderson Gibbs gave back much to the community she loved. She was without a doubt a link back to the beginnings as an American social conscience, a tribute to the women who came before her, and an inspiration to those who came after.

The "Anderson Factor" is the thread of strength uniting three generations of women in divergent times.

❧

PRESERVING THE CITY GATE
Women at the Front (1900)

St. Augustine's City Gate was in danger of being demolished as the town eased into the twentieth century. A rapidly growing cedar tree and an unsympathetic City Council threatened to end the days of the twin towers. However, the disaster was averted by two groups of tenacious and feisty ladies. The Daughters of the American Revolution (DAR) and the National Society of Colonial Dames of America in the State of Florida separately and staunchly fought to preserve the statuesque columns with the stone abutments and double sentry boxes.

The masonry pillars that once supported a gate were constructed in 1808 by Royal Engineer Manuel de Hita as part of an improved defense system. The original system consisted of a moat and a wall constructed of earth and palm logs. It ran west from the Castillo de San Marcos to the San Sebastian River. The western edge of town was similarly protected with a wall extending from north to south. The defense system built during the years after Governor Moore's raid of 1702 included a gate allowing access to the city only during daylight hours. Sentries manned the gate and stood watch from the numerous redoubts projecting from the walls.

Over the years the British and the returning Spanish restored and maintained the walls, the bridge, and the City Gate. The Spanish embellished the work of the British by strengthening the wall and widening the moat to forty feet. It was during the Second Spanish Period that a nine-foot-high earthwork wall was added and prickly Spanish bayonet foliage planted for further defense.

By the 1900s, all that remained of the "gate" were two pillars with portions of the wall and two sentry boxes. It was no longer of any defensive value, but the ladies of the town were greatly disturbed by threats of its destruction. It was, they felt, a picturesque addition to the historic town and should not be removed.

The first protests came from members of the Daughters of the American Revolution. An article in the society newspaper *Tatler* in 1900 reports:

> The (Maria Jefferson) chapter has taken up the work of preserving the City Gate, and has forwarded to the Secretary of State, through Captain Charles McKinstry, a request to have it repaired and

*to take steps to prevent further demolition. There can be no question of
the necessity for this work, but the recommendations that the trees growing on top of the abutments (be destroyed) has provoked a great deal
of discussion.*

The article emphasizes either the trees be sacrificed or the relics of
the gate removed. In the view of the author of the article, all efforts must
be made to support the ladies of the DAR in their quest to save the
City Gate.

Their hand-written minutes attest to their efforts.

Minutes of the Daughters of the American Revolution
(DAR), January 24, 1900:

*The preservation of the City Gates[1] was discussed and a com-
mittee was appointed to see Capt. McKinstry and try to get him to use
his influence to get one congressman to have something done to preserve
them. Mrs. Dismukes and Miss Anna Everett were put on that committee.*

Minutes of the DAR, February 14, 1900:

*The report of the committee, Mrs. Dismukes and Miss Anna
Everett on the City Gates was read by Miss Anna Everett who
reported as their having interviewed Capt. McKinstry who said he
would give every help in his power and forward the committee's letter
to the proper authorities with his recommendation for immediate attention to the City Gates and so preserve one of the oldest landmarks in
the country.*

Oral history as written in Karen Harvey's *St. Augustine and St. Johns
County: A Pictorial History,* reports:

*At about this time three ladies, Elizabeth (Mrs. John) Dismukes,
Annie (Mrs. Thomas) Woodruff and Rosalie (Mrs. Josiah) James,
dressed in mourning clothes and "with black veils flowing in the
breeze, served tea beside the wall until further consideration was given
to saving the historic structure."*

Frequently the legend states they "chained themselves to the walls,"
but the ladies much preferred a genteel tea party to such dramatics. And,
most importantly, their tactics worked.

Years later it became the challenge of the Colonial Dames to aid in
the preservation of the City Gate. Their self-appointed task was to affix

- Circa 1900 -
Gift to NPS from
Colonial Dames of America in

A family stops before the City Gate around 1900 when demolition was considered. (Photo from collection of Bureau of Archives and Records Management, Florida Department of State)

a tablet to the gate stating its history. The first stumbling block was the difficulty in unearthing information about the early years of the defense system. Research began in 1903 and continued for three years.

Finally a description of the gate was sent to Cabaret and Company in New York with a request to submit a design in keeping with the gate's Moorish architecture. All did not go smoothly, however. A *St. Augustine Record* article covering the 1972 unveiling of a new plaque described the problems encountered as revealed in a speech by Miss Dana Snodgrass of the Colonial Dames Board of Managers.

Harkening back to the struggles of the early 1900s she said, "In due time a design was received. It was decorated with a conventional border of daisies and leaves, one and a half inches wide, utterly inappropriate and entirely without dignity. It did not suggest the Spanish or Moorish (styles) and was rejected. It was returned to Cabaret and Company with the criticism and they were requested to try again."

After some discussion, a working design was prepared based on a print of a Moorish floral design from Spain's Alhambra Palace. The ladies sent it back to the company with hopes of dedication in 1906. However, the difficulties had not ended. The plaque arrived with the word *coquina* misspelled. Coquina, from which the pillars were constructed, is a compacted shell stone indigenous to Florida. It was used by the Spanish for construction of wells, buildings, and the unconquerable fort, the Castillo de San Marcos. It was imperative that the word, so meaningful to the history of the town, was spelled right. By the time the correction was made and the tablet returned, the date was April 3, 1907. The date on the tablet though read 1906. Wisely the ladies deemed that to be acceptable and proceeded with the dedication.

The 1907 plaque read, "These gates were begun as a defense against the English in 1743 during the reign of King Philip V of Spain. In 1804 they were rebuilt of coquina by Antonio Arredondo, Royal Engineer of Spain. This tablet is erected by the National Society of Colonial Dames of America resident in Florida, 1906."

The society was pleased until further information was uncovered by the National Park Service. The Park Service became custodian of the City Gate in 1933. In the 1960s they did extensive historical research and determined the information on the plaque was inaccurate. A new flurry of excitement swept the town as it was revealed that credit should be given to Royal Engineer Manuel de Hita, not Antonio Arredondo. The date of construction was changed from 1804 to 1808. The date attributed to the establishment of the early defense system was adjusted from 1743 to 1739. A *Florida Times-Union* article of 1972 boldly proclaimed: *"Old City Gate Tablet Wrong."*[2]

With good-natured resignation, the findings of the Park Service were accepted by the Colonial Dames and a new plaque was ordered. They decided to make the rededication a special event at the Castillo de San Marcos Tricentennial Celebration in 1972. The ceremony commemorated the November 9, 1672, date of the laying of the fort's cornerstone. Miss Snodgrass defused the embarrassment of their errors by beginning her speech, "From time immemorial women have changed their minds. And you and I know that no reason is reason enough." She proceeded to explain that 325 members of the National Society (of Colonial Dames) have "reasons good and proper for a reversal of past decisions." It had taken nearly three-quarters of a century to rectify the error, but it was completed with pride and dignity.[3]

The new text reads: THIS GATE, OPENED IN 1739, PROVIDED THE ONLY ACCESS THROUGH THE DEFENSE LINE ON THE NORTH SIDE OF SPANISH ST. AUGUSTINE. ROYAL ENGINEER MANUEL DE HITA BUILT THESE COQUINA PILLARS IN 1808. THIS TABLET WAS ORIGINALLY ERECTED IN 1907 BY THE NATIONAL SOCIETY OF THE COLONIAL DAMES OF AMERICA IN THE STATE OF FLORIDA. IT WAS REVISED TO COMMEMORATE THE TRICENTENNIAL OF CASTILLO DE SAN MARCOS. 1972.

Through the efforts of the women of DAR and Colonial Dames, St.

Augustine still has its two-story coquina columns capped by stone pomegranates intact. Visitors and residents pass through the City Gate daily. Few, however, realize how fortunate we are still to have our proud pillars from the past.

CHAPTER VIII

Contemporary Trail Blazers

❧

THE FAMOUS FIRSTS IN AMERICA'S FIRST CITY

There is a simple beauty in being first. No one else can achieve that goal. Others might be smarter, richer, or better—but never first. The list of women who achieved a "first" in the ranks of male-dominated positions in St. Augustine includes the first newspaper editor, first judge, first mayor, first deputy sheriff, and first city police patrol sergeant.

❧

NINA HAWKINS
First Female Newspaper Editor

The first female newspaper editor was Nina Hawkins whose journalism career started at the *St. Augustine Record* in 1910 when she was twenty-one years of age. She continued in her field for forty-three years, nineteen of those as editor-in-chief. When she was appointed editor in 1934, it gave her the distinction of becoming the first woman editor of a daily newspaper in the state of Florida.

Hawkins' first beat was as a society reporter, the only reasonable place to start a woman in that day. However, a society reporter covered more than the local coffee-klatches and social gatherings. St. Augustine was still a hotel town back in the mid-1930s then with numerous rich and famous personalities visiting the elegant Ponce de León and popular Alcazar and Cordova Hotels, not to mention the Florida House and Magnolia Hotel of downtown fame.

It wasn't a bad job for a woman—particularly when you realize women didn't even have the right to vote until 1919. And Hawkins was right for the job. She was an adept writer and observer who maintained a consistency within the newspaper during a career spanning two wars and a Florida real estate boom and bust before quietly retiring during the innocuous mid-century years of the 1950s.

Hawkins' keen sense of responsibility may have resulted from the influence of her mother who raised three children as a widowed single parent. Laura Hawkins brought her children to St. Augustine from Lake George, Florida, when Nina was twelve. She earned her salary as a schoolteacher.

Although not a St. Augustine native, Nina Hawkins' love for the city burgeoned when preservation efforts surfaced under the guidance of Mayor Walter B. Fraser. Fraser launched the first restoration program getting the attention of the Carnegie Institution of Washington, D.C. The restoration committee appointed by the mayor in 1937 consisted of United States Senator Scott M. Loftin, Judge David R. Dunham, Carl W. Hawkins, president of Model Land Company, a subsidiary of the Henry M. Flagler interests, and Nina Hawkins. Carl Hawkins was Nina's brother. The Restoration Edition of the *Record* won the state award as the outstanding paper of its circulation class for that year.

Nina Hawkins was good at her job in many ways. The list of service organizations she belonged to or supported included Colonial Dames of America, Daughters of the American Revolution, Florida State Historical Society, Woman's Exchange, The King's Daughters, American Red Cross, Flagler Hospital Auxiliary, and Cherokee Garden Club. Her honors included life membership with the Florida Women's Press Club, the Florida Press Association's award for editing the most outstanding newspaper in its circulation class, and St. Augustine Historical Society award for outstanding contributions. Her most recent honor came in 1999 when she was posthumously inducted into the Florida Press Association's Hall of Fame as its twenty-eighth member.

Nina Hawkins' reputation for maintaining strict editorial policies and demanding meticulous writing is exemplified in a story about a reporter called into Hawkins' office and told to sit down. Knowing he had committed an error he awaited her pronouncement.

"Thomas," she firmly chided. "You have split an infinitive."[1]

Nothing can better describe the charm, dedication, and wit of editor-in-chief Nina Hawkins. "Miss Nina," as she was called, died in St. Augustine in 1972 at the age of eighty-two.

❦

EVELYN HAMBLEN
First Female School Board Member

Evelyn Hamblen Center is nestled alongside Oyster Creek just out of sight of the heavily-traveled roads off U.S. Route 1. The little school opened in 1925 as West Augustine Grammar School with one class for each grade level from one through six. Its evolution included a change to West Augustine Elementary School before the 1957 dedication of the school to educator Evelyn Hamblen.

Few students at the Evelyn Hamblen Elementary School knew much about her and today, as the Evelyn Hamblen Alternative Center for academically at-risk children, even fewer know of her reputation as a political advocate for the school system in St. Johns County.

Miss Hamblen, born in 1874 in Bangor, Maine, arrived in St. Augustine in 1900. She was a public school educator for many years, best known for teaching Latin and English at St. Augustine High School. After retirement Miss Hamblen went on to become a member of the school board. Her position as the board's first female chairperson gave her the distinction of becoming St. Johns County's first female elected school board official. Miss Hamblen served until her death in 1943.

Miss Hamblen's obituary in the *St. Augustine Record* of September 19, 1943, states in the headline that schools will close. The article notes schools, both white and colored, would be closed in the city (St. Augustine) and in Hastings and Mill Creek (outlying communities) permitting the teachers and others desiring to do so to attend the funeral. That is testimony to her dedication to the public school system.[2]

❦

PEGGY READY
First Female County Court Judge

"First judge" Peggy Ready drove to St. Augustine fresh out of law school to visit friends in December 1979. She had not yet taken her bar exam as she was unsure of where she wanted to settle. She drove into St. Augustine and the decision was made.

"The only building put up since the '40s was Kmart," she joyfully remembered about the small, historic town. Instead of returning to South Carolina where she obtained her juris doctor degree from the

University of South Carolina, she moved to St. Augustine. She studied Florida law, passed the bar exam, and took her oath of office in May 1980. She began her legal career as an assistant public defender, later chief of that department, then moved into private practice, and finally became an assistant state attorney before her judicial appointment as a St. Johns County Court Judge in January 1990. As St. Augustine is the

1. Nina Hawkins, Editor
2. Evelyn Hamblen, Educator
3. Peggy Ready, Judge
4. Ramelle Petroglou, Mayor
5. Peggy Caraway Cottle, Deputy Sheriff
6. Michele Perry, Police Sergeant

county seat of St. Johns County, this position kept Ready in or near the city of her choice.

Becoming the first "lady" judge was, she admitted, a bit daunting but it wasn't the first "first" for her by any means. After graduation from college, the Arkansas-born and Mississippi-raised adventurer began a life of "firsts" by heading to Korea with the American Red Cross in support of overseas forces. After a year as a "Doughnut Dolly," Ready settled in New York City to try her wings as a playwright but found that was not her calling. A second tour with Red Cross—this time in Europe—led to the decision to become active in the military instead of remaining in a support position to the armed forces. She joined the Women's Army Corps (WAC) as a first lieutenant in 1965. The following year she became the first WAC commander in Vietnam. She commanded ninety-five women and found the experience one of the greatest jobs she ever had.[3] For her service in Vietnam she was awarded the Bronze Star, a military medal for meritorious service, the first of several medals she would receive during her military career.

After Vietnam, Ready found herself embroiled in controversy rather than combat. Her assignment as commander of a four hundred–woman WAC company at Ft. Gordon, Georgia, came during a time when gender issues were surfacing. Ready was faced with the dilemma of dealing with disciplinary problems when the Army had not formulated a policy for detaining women before discharging them. Ready said women could not be put in jail or the stockade, so they remained in the WAC detachment area. She had to find male noncommissioned officers to act as guards until the women could be officially dismissed from duty. She dealt with the situation calling it a "tough assignment."

Ready remained in the Army on active duty until age thirty-five when she decided to pursue a career in the legal field. She did not, however, shelve her military career. She joined the Army Reserve Command and became the first woman commandant of a Reserve school. In addition to the Bronze Star she received the Meritorious Service Medal, Army Commendation Medal, three Vietnam-related medals, and a variety of reserve service medals. She retired from service in 1993 with the rank of full colonel.

In 1990 Ready was appointed county court judge in St. Johns County—the first female so chosen. Judge Ready served in that capacity until her retirement in March 2000.

Ready distinguished herself in the role of first female judge in St. Johns County. Her achievements in the military service and throughout her law career make her a woman of many famous firsts.

❧

RAMELLE PETROGLOU
First Female Mayor

Ramelle Petroglou did not—and still does not—fit the image of an official in a town known for its "good ol' boy" politics. The sweet-faced, ever-smiling woman doesn't appear to be tough enough for the rigors of leadership in an all-male arena. But she proved she could play the game—and win it.

Petroglou functioned as a St. Augustine city commissioner from 1978 to 1981. At that time the commissioners selected the mayor from their ranks and she was chosen by her peers for the leadership position. Unfortunately not everyone was ready for a female mayor and six months before completion of her term there was a coup attempt by one of her fellow commissioners. However, the action to remove Petroglou as mayor created a furor in town precipitating a change in the selection procedure. As her two-year term came to an end, the mayoral seat became an elected position allowing the mayor to be chosen by popular vote for the first time. Petroglou ran for the office on a platform of citizen involvement and open government and won the 1983 race.

Petroglou fulfilled the term as mayor and remains the only female mayor in the history of St. Augustine. While Petroglou said she was always treated "just like one of the guys" she also noted she believes more women should get involved in politics. She said women "probably are a lot more sensitive to community needs then men are."[4]

Perhaps that is true. She proved a woman not only could do the job, but she changed the way the city chose the person to uphold that office.

An accounting of accomplishments during her years in service include annexation of Anastasia State Recreation Area, facilitating the building of a new public library, and restructuring the heart of town by making historic St. George Street a pedestrian-only thoroughfare from the City Gate to the Plaza de la Constitución.

Although Petroglou abandoned politics on a personal level, the last six years of a thirty-year career as a civilian employee with the Florida National Guard kept her in close touch with government work. Her job as executive assistant for legislative affairs for the Guard required frequent travel to Florida's capital Tallahassee. She retired from employment with the National Guard in 1994 choosing to fill her days with projects in an artistic realm which had eluded her during her active years in a career and in political life.

Today the mayoral role remains an elected position. Whether or not Petroglou decides to actively enter politics again, she has made her mark as the first female mayor and the one responsible for changing the rules of the game.

※

PEGGY CARAWAY COTTLE
First Female Deputy Sheriff

A 1975 graduate of Flagler College, Peggy Caraway was unsure of where a bachelor's degree in social sciences would take her. Thinking law enforcement might be interesting she arranged for an interview with Dudley Garrett, then sheriff of St. Johns County. She mentioned to him she didn't think some laws were fair—like why should someone be arrested just for carrying a joint or two in his pocket? That question almost lost her the first job out of college, but instead it instilled in her the realization that you don't decide which laws you will or will not uphold.

Caraway attended an intensive six-month basic law enforcement course at St. Augustine Technical Center (now First Coast Technical Center) before working as a member of the St. Johns County Sheriff's Office Reserves. In September of 1976 Caraway became a full time detention officer at the St. Johns County Jail and one year later joined the Sheriff's Patrol Division thus becoming the first female deputy sheriff in St. Johns County Sheriff's Patrol Division.

Being a "first" was a stepping stone for Caraway, who later married John Cottle. She earned a masters degree in criminal justice from Rollins College, Winter Park, Florida, and spent eight years working in the law enforcement field in St. Augustine.

Today Peggy Cottle works at the University of Florida as a secretary in a residence hall. She admits to becoming "burned out" with law enforcement and is now content with a more relaxing job.

※

MICHELE PERRY
First Female City Police Sergeant

Michele Perry is a woman of determination. She had to buck her own father's wishes to reach the goal of becoming the first female patrol sergeant in the St. Augustine Police Department. It wasn't that Michele's father disliked the law enforcement profession—quite the contrary. Her father Neil Perry was elected sheriff of St. Johns County in 1985 and successfully won the office in every election since that time.

Perry said she knew she wanted to be in law enforcement from a very young age—from second grade, to be exact. It continued to be her dream throughout high school, but marriage took precedence for awhile. Then in 1991 when she was ready to enter the law enforcement field she ran into a speed bump—her father. First there was the issue of nepotism. If she worked in the sheriff's department she would never be promoted, nor could she be assigned to specialized teams involving monetary compensations. So she decided she wanted to join the Police Department. But this is when her father balked. He advised against a career in the field because it was "a very harsh career and a male-dominated field."

Perry moved ahead despite the warnings. But she admitted it was not always easy. She said it took a long time to build up confidence with her male counterparts. She estimated that it took about a year and a half to gain their respect noting that some women never reach that point. She said, "What you have to do is become one of the guys."

On a scale of one to ten with males on one end of the spectrum and females on the other, Perry has hit every number. She worked as a "drug cop" making arrests in dangerous drug-saturated neighborhoods. She worked on stings to capture would-be thieves. And she worked as an undercover hooker. No, she said, she didn't wear a miniskirt and heels. She dressed in ragged jeans and baggy shirts to look like the hookers in the target neighborhood. Yes she was approached but, she said, "I had backup officers."

She also became the first woman to patrol on bicycle. She said she really liked that because she was able to meet people in the downtown area and talk with them. The presence of police did, she said, deter crime on the downtown streets.

After a year of bike patrol she went back to patrol work. In 1997 when she had been on the force for six years she was promoted to patrol supervisor, making history as the first female in that position. Perry's supervisory duties encompass internal affairs responsibilities, training supervision, and records supervision.

Perhaps she did become "one of the guys," but Perry never lost the feminine touch. She never forgets birthdays or Christmas. She said it is the little things that make them think, "Hey, I have someone who cares," noting it doesn't take that much time out of the day to go get a birthday card. She added, "It means a lot to them. I bring things to my department that have never been done before."

Perry is not afraid to go the extra mile as a woman. She said it all when she said, "Females have brought into law enforcement a gentler touch."

And what about her father?

"He is very proud," Perry acknowledged.

And what about her future?

"How about first female chief of police?" she said. Why not?

Undoubtedly there are more trail blazers and many others will surface in time. There are people like Phyllis Lydon who became the first female chairman—or is it chair*woman* or chair*person* or simply chair—of the St. Johns County Commission in 1986. In serving her two-year-term she paved the road for other female "chairs."

Betsy Haynes is credited with being the first female lawyer in town. Betsy has since left the legal field after a successful career to move on with a new calling. She earned a master of divinity and a master of theology from Princeton Theological Seminary, Princeton, New Jersey. She was ordained as a minister in February 2002 and is now the pastor of Northside Presbyterian Church in Jacksonville, Florida. When asked about the significance of being a "first" during an interview in July 2001, Haynes shrugged and remarked, "That was 25 years ago!" Perhaps she plans another first as well.

Debbie Mull created quite a stir in St. Augustine as the first female proprietor of a carpentry business. She owned and operated Debbie's Kitchen Cabinets in the late 1970s and early 1980s. Her responsibilities included measuring counters and walls for fit, presenting cost estimates, selling the jobs, and creating final drawings. All considered at the time "man's work." Debbie's expertise opened the door to her appointment as CEO of the St. Johns County Builders Council.

Another female first is Sharon Holmes who was the first woman to serve as director of engineering for St. Johns County, Florida. In 1998 Sharon moved to Tallahassee to become the state maintenance engineer. Sharon works closely with Christine Speer, the first female director of maintenance for Florida's DOT. Both Sharon and Christine share maintenance duties for the state of Florida.

Karen Taylor wasn't just the first, she was the *only* land planner for St. Johns County, a position she filled in her "one-person planning office" in 1980. She now owns her own land-planning business which is fine, she said, "if you approve of planning and development."

In a world where so many women are oppressed, we in the United States should be proud to say in the twenty-first century we hardly notice female firsts. Firsts were necessary to pave the uncharted roads. But now the doors are wide open as the women of St. Augustine have certainly demonstrated. It is up to each individual to walk through them.

CONCLUSION

The tragedy of September 11, 2001, awakened the western world to the atrocities inflicted on some Islamic women. In *Buried Alive*, award-winning journalist Jane Goodwin writes that until the Taliban came to power, Saudi Arabia was the most oppressive country on earth for women. As the story of the horrors inflicted upon the women of Afghanistan surfaced, the western world was outraged.

In *Price of Honor*, Goodwin writes of the plight of a young girl immersed in the Muslim culture. She knew the girl had been beaten badly but the girl's grandmother told her a man has the right to beat the women in his family. She had been robbed of an education and Goodwin was advised that education is bad for girls because it makes them argumentative and unmarriageable. The girl was removed from Goodwin's influence and at the age of eleven forced into marriage with an abusive man.

Until September 11, 2001, the western world went blithely about its business, oblivious to the atrocities committed against women in the Islamic nations. Certainly Afghanistan, while under the rule of the Taliban, is the most overt example of injustice to women in the modern world.

In the United States when a delegation of women wrote the Declaration of Sentiments in 1848[1] they patterned the words after those written by men for the Declaration of Independence. It was a conscious move to demonstrate that in this country women have the same rights as men. The result of that movement was gaining the right to vote with ratification of the Nineteenth Amendment to the constitution in 1919.

In a perfect world all humans are created equal. But this isn't a perfect world and men and women often struggle with adversity. The women presented as the *Daring Daughters* found a way to live their lives as they desired. Some overcame obstacles, some created their own roadblocks. All of them survived.

ENDNOTES

CHAPTER I
Antonia
1. Solís de Merás. *Pedro Menèndez de Avilès*, p. 190.
2. Gannon. *A New History of Florida*, p. 17.

Manuela de Mier Mickler
1. Griffin. *Mullet on the Beach*, p. 25.
2. Mickler, Patricia. *The Micklers of Florida*, p. 123.
3. *El Escribano*. Coles and Waters, p. 37.

CHAPTER II
Maria Andreu
1. Information was supplied by the staff of the St. Augustine Lighthouse and Museum, Inc., and from a video of St. Augustine storyteller Diana Rooks.

Lola Sanchez
1. Interviews with descendants Carol Bradshaw and Shirley Browning.

Kat Twine
1. Information and quotes from interviews with Katherine "Kat" Twine by Nadia Reardon appearing in the July 3, 2001, issue of *Folio* Magazine and with Karen Harvey printed in the Compass section of the *St. Augustine Record*, February 25, 1988.
2. Both Kat and Henry Twine were honored in 1992 with a park in Lincolnville on Lovett Street. The Great Floridian 2000 marker was placed in the Twine yard on January 19, 2002, in honor of Mr. Twine's achievements.

CHAPTER III
Mary Evans
1. The name *David* was a fictitious name given by author Eugenia Price.
2. Griffin. *Mullet On the Beach*, p. 4.
3. 1784 Census, St. Augustine Historical Society Research Library.
4. Price. *Maria*, p. 351.
5. Griffin, p. 15.

Anna Kingsley
1. The date of 1803 rather than 1806 is given by Bennett *(Twelve on the River St. Johns*, p. 90) as the year Kingsley returned to St. Augustine with his wife Anna Madgigene Jai. Blakey, in *Parade of Memories*, verifies purchases made by Kingsley in St. Augustine on November 26, 1803, but says nothing about Anna. Although the land purchases place Kingsley in St. Augustine in 1803, it does not prove Anna was in Florida. According to the manumission document of March 4, 1811, Anna was about eighteen years of age when given her freedom and her first child George was three years and nine months old. It is far more reasonable to believe the date of 1806 as the year of her arrival in Florida and marriage with George's birth following in 1807.
2. Schafer. *Anna Kingsley*. Schafer states Kingsley was born in Bristol, England. The Gibbs family (see Watt's family history) claim Scottish ancestry.
3. Schafer. p. 38.

Abbie Brooks
1. Punnett, Dick. *East Florida Gazette*, February 1999, p. 4.
2. Brooks. *Petals Plucked From Sunny Climes*, p. 231.
3. Punnett. *East Florida Gazette*, p. 8.
4. *Ibid.*

5. Pope, Margo C. "The Abby Brooks Saga," from Owene Weber's graveside eulogy in *St. Augustine Record*, November 12, 2000.
6. Waterbury, Jean Parker. *East-Florida Gazette*, February 1999, p. 9.
7. Punnett. *East Florida Gazette*, p. 6.
8. Punnett. *East Florida Gazette*, p. 7.
9. Telephone interview with Yvonne Punnett, February 4, 2000.

CHAPTER IV
Dominga de Zéspedes
1. Tanner, Helen Hornbeck. *Zéspedes in East Florida, 1784–1790.* Preface to the 1989 edition, xv.
2. Tanner. p. 76.

Catalina Morain
1. The story of the Delaney murder case appears in Tanner's *Zéspedes in East Florida, 1784–1790,* and in an extended version in pamphlet form written by Tanner on file in the St. Augustine Historical Society Research Library files.
2. Archivist Bruce Chappell of the University of Florida was told of the deathbed confession by fellow archivist Daniel Ross. Ross found the document in the *Papeles de Cuba,* a collection of papers within the Archives of the Indies in Seville, Spain. Although Chappel has never viewed the document, he does not doubt Ross's discovery.

CHAPTER V
Ximénez-Fatio House
1. *East Florida Gazette*, November 24, 1821; Waterbury. *The Ximénez-Fatio House*, p. 10; St. Johns County Deed Books B & L, p. 96.
2. St. Johns County Deed Book F, p. 141.
3. Robert E. Nichols completed research on the Whitehurst/Cook relationship and deduced that both women had the same mother. No document proves they were sisters but age and place of birth indicate they were. Information about the Whitehurst, Cook, and Gerty families can be found in the monograph by Robert Nichols on file at the St. Augustine Historical Society Research Library.
4. Dr. Peck's Ledger, No. 39, St. Augustine Historical Society Research Library.
5. Waterbury. *Ximénez-Fatio House*, p. 21; Dowell, I., p. 387.

Lucy Abbott
1. Document found in St. Augustine Historical Society file.

Luella Day McConnell
1. McConnell's speech, miscellaneous letters, newspaper articles, and documents can be found in the files of the St. Augustine Historical Society Research Library.
2. Historical Society files. Letter dated March 25, 1950, attention Mrs. Moulds.
3. Letter from Ian Whitaker, St. Augustine Institute of Science, to Librarian, July 14, 1978.
4. Monteau. St. Augustine Historical Society files.
5. *St. Augustine Record*, April 19, 1901.
6. "First Encounters" on the Fountain of Youth grounds is an exhibit of the Florida Museum of Natural History and The University of Florida. It is scripted by Dr. Susan Milbrath and Jerald Milanich.
7. *Florida Today*, December 16, 1991.
8. Letter to W. J. Harris, St. Augustine Historical Society from Emily Wilson, July 10, 1929.

CHAPTER VI
Flagler's Women
1. Akin, p. 6; Bible verse Matthew 25: 14–30.
2. Chandler. *The Binghams of Louisville*, p. 98.
3. St. Johns County Deed Book 22, filed June 20, 1911.
4. Chandler. *The Binghams of Louisville*, p. 111.
5. *St. Augustine Record*, May 31, 1937.
6. Chandler. *Henry Flagler*, p. 264.

CHAPTER VII
Sarah Mather and Rebecca Perit

1. *Tatler,* February 18, 1893, p. 13.
2. Ibid. January 21, 1892.
3. The *St. Augustine Evening Record,* May 6, 1901, p. 2.

The Anderson Factor

1. Waterbury. *Ximénez-Fatio House,* p. 11.
2. Graham. *The Awakening of St. Augustine,* p. 75.
3. Waterbury. *The Treasurer's House,* p. 70.
4. Graham. *The Awakening of St. Augustine,* p. 84.
5. Graham, p. 115.
6. Waterbury. *The Treasurer's House,* p. 38, p. 40; Graham, p. 120.
7. Interview with Mary Gibbs Smethurst Grant; Watt, p. 31.
8. Graham, p. 204.
9. Graham, p. 213.
10. Interview with George W. Gibbs IV.

Preserving the City Gate

1. City Gate is singular—one gate. The plural form is written when "City Gates" is used in a quote. The plural form was a common practice in past years referring to two pillars.
2. *Florida Times-Union* article by Nancy Powell.
3. *St. Augustine Record* article by Anne Carling.

CHAPTER VIII
Contemporary Trail Blazers

1. *East Florida Gazette,* July 1981.
2. Information supplied by Paul Abbati-nozzi, principal of Evelyn Hamblen Center.
3. Article by Major Doni Houghton, Chief of Information Services for the Public Affairs Office, Headquarters, Second U.S. Army, November 1990.
4. Interview with author, 2001.

CONCLUSION

1. The Seneca Falls Women's Rights Convention was held in New York in July 1848. The document is credited to Elizabeth Cady Stanton who was one of several women's rights advocates.

BIBLIOGRAPHY

Akin, Edward N. *Flagler: Rockefeller Partner and Florida Baron*. Kent, Ohio: Kent State University Press, 1988.

Arana, Luis. "Defenses and Defenders at St. Augustine." *El Escribano: The St. Augustine Journal of History*, Vol. 36 (1999).

Arana, Luis and Albert Manucy. *The Building of Castillo de San Marcos*. Eastern National Park and Monument Association for Castillo de San Marcos National Monument, 1977.

Barrientos, Bartolomé. *Pedro Menéndez de Avilés: Founder of Florida*. Gainesville: University Press of Florida, 1965. Facsimile reproduction of the sole edition of the original Spanish work written in 1567.

Bennett, Charles E. *Twelve on the River St. Johns*. Gainesville: University Press of Florida, 1989.

Blakey, Arch Frederic. *Parade of Memories: A History of Clay County, Florida*. Clay County Bicentennial Steering Committee. Jacksonville, Florida: Drummand Press, 1976.

The Branches: Springs of Living Water. One Hundred Years of a Florida Parish, 1875–1975. Green Cove Springs, Florida: Emerald Printing Company, 1975.

Brenner, Marie. *House of Dreams, The Bingham Family of Louisville*. New York: Random House, 1988.

Brooks, Abbie. *Petals Plucked from Sunny Climes*. Gainesville: University Presses of Florida, 1976. Facsimile reproduction of the 1880 edition. (Originally published under pseudonym Silvia Sunshine.)

_____. *The Unwritten History of Old St. Augustine*. Copied from the Spanish Archives in Seville, Spain. Translated by Annie Averette. St. Augustine: St. Augustine Record Company, 1907.

Chandler, David Leon. *Henry Flagler: The Astonishing Life and Times of the Visionary Robber Baron Who Founded Florida*. New York: MacMillan, 1986.

Chandler, David Leon with Mary Voelz Chandler. *The Binghams of Louisville. The Dark History Behind One of America's Great Fortunes*. New York: Crown Publishers, 1987.

Chernow, Ron. *Titan: The Life of John D. Rockefeller, Sr.* New York: Vintage Books, 1998.

Child, Lydia Maria. *Letters from New York*. New York: Third Edition. Books for Libraries, 1970.

Colburn, David R. *Racial Change and Community Crisis: St. Augustine, Florida, 1877–1980*. New York: Columbia University Press, 1985.

Colburn, David R. and Jane L. Landers. *The African American Heritage of Florida*. Gainesville: University Press of Florida, 1995.

Coles, David J. and Zack C. Waters. "Indian Fighter, Confederate Soldier, Blockade Runner, and Scout: The Life and Letters of Jacob E. Mickler." *El Escribano: The St. Augustine Journal of History.* St. Augustine, Florida, 1997.

Day, Luella. *The Tragedy of the Klondike.* New York: Self-published, 1906.

Dowell, J. E. *Florida Historic, Dramatic, Contemporary.* New York: Lewis Historical Publications Company, 1952.

Gannon, Michael, ed. *A New History of Florida.* Gainesville: University Press of Florida, 1996.

Goodwin, Jan. *Buried Alive: Afghan Women Under the Taliban.* On Issues, Summer 1998, Vol. 7, No. 3. Web page: 7–2–98, 1998.

_____. *Price of Honor: Muslim Women Lift the Veil of Silence on the Islamic World.* New York: Plume Books, 1994.

Graham, Thomas. *The Awakening of St. Augustine: The Anderson Family and the Oldest City: 1821–1924.* St. Augustine, Florida: St. Augustine Historical Society, 1978.

Griffin, Patricia C. *Mary Evans: A Woman of Substance.* St. Augustine, Florida: *El Escribano: St. Augustine Historical Society*, 1977.

_____. *Mullet On the Beach: The Minorcans of Florida 1768–1788.* Jacksonville: University of North Florida Press, 1991.

Harvey, Karen. *St. Augustine and St. Johns County: A Pictorial History.* Norfolk, Virginia: Donning Company Publishers, 1980.

_____. *Flagler Hospital: A Gift of Life.* St. Augustine, Florida: Community Relations Department of Flagler Hospital, 1989.

_____. *Florida's First Presbyterians: A Celebration of 175 Years in St. Augustine, 1824–1999.* St. Augustine, Florida: Memorial Presbyterian Church, 1998.

Hann, John H. *A History of the Timucua Indians and Missions.* Gainesville: University Press of Florida, 1996.

In the White Man's Image (Video). Nebraska ETV Network/University of Nebraska-Lincoln Television and the Native American Public Broadcasting Consortium. Produced by Christine Lesiak with Nebraska ETV and Matthew Jones for NAPBC, 1992.

Landers, Jane. *Black Society in Spanish Florida.* Chicago: University of Illinois Press, 1999.

Lyon, Eugene. *Richer Than We Thought: The Material Culture of Sixteenth-Century St. Augustine.* St. Augustine, Florida. *El Escribano. The St. Augustine Journal of History*, 1992.

Manucy, Albert. *Florida's Menéndez: Captain General of the Ocean Sea.* Sarasota, Florida: Pineapple Press, 1992.

Martin, Sidney Walter. *Florida's Flagler.* Athens: University of Georgia Press, 1949.

McCarthy, Kevin M., ed. *The Book Lover's Guide to Florida.* Sarasota, Florida: Pineapple Press, 1992.

McGoun, William E. *Prehistoric Peoples of South Florida.* Tuscaloosa: The University of Alabama Press, 1993.

Mayer, Melanie J. *Klondike Women: True Tales of the 1897–98 Gold Rush.* Athens: Ohio University Press, 1989.

Mickler, Latrell E. *Indigo.* Xlibras Corporation. www.Xlibris.com, 2000.

_____. Patricia Ferguson. *The Micklers of Florida.* Chuluota, Florida: Mickler House, Publishers, 1991.

Milanich, Jerald T. *Florida Indians and the Invasion from Europe.* Gainesville: University Press of Florida, 1995.

Milanich, Jerald T. and Susan Milbrath, eds. *First Encounters: Spanish Explorations in the Caribbean and the United States, 1492–1570.* Gainesville: University of Florida Press, 1989.

Mowet, Charles L. *East Florida as a British Province, 1763–1784.* Los Angeles:

University of California Press, 1943. Facsimile reproduction. Gainesville: University of Florida Press, 1964.

Nolan, David. *Fifty Feet In Paradise. The Booming of Florida.* New York: Harcourt Brace Jovanovitch,1984.

Pratt, Richard Henry. *Battlefield and Classroom: Four Decades with the American Indian, 1867–1904.* Lincoln: University of Nebraska Press, 1964. Copyright 1964 by Robert M. Utley, ed.

Price, Eugenia. *Maria.* New York: J. B. Lippincott Company, 1977.

Quinn, Jane. *Minorcans in Florida: Their History and Heritage.* St. Augustine, Florida: Mission Press, 1975.

Schafer, Daniel L. *Anna Kingsley, Revised and Expanded Edition.* St. Augustine, Florida: St. Augustine Historical Society, 1997.

Solís de Merás, Gonzalo. *Pedro Menéndez de Avilés.* Facsimile reproduction. Gainesville: Univeristy of Florida Press, 1964.

Sunshine, Silvia. See Brooks, Abbie.

Tanner, Helen Hornbeck. *Zéspedes In East Florida 1784–1790.* Jacksonville: University of North Florida Press, 1963.

_____. "The Delaney Murder Case." Pamphlet printed by the St. Augustine Historical Society. In Research Library files.

Waterbury, Jean Parker. *Markland.* St. Augustine, Florida: St. Augustine Historical Society, 1989.

_____. *The Treasurer's House.* St. Augustine, Florida: St. Augustine Historical Society, 1994.

_____. *The Ximénez-Fatio House: Long Neglected, Now Restored.* St. Augustine Historical Society, 1985.

Watt, Margaret Gibbs. *The Gibbs Family of Long Ago and Near At Hand.*

Jacksonville: Self-published, 1967.

NEWSPAPERS

East Florida Gazette
Florida Times Union
Florida Today
St. Augustine Evening News
St. Augustine Evening Record
St. Augustine Record
Tatler

ST. AUGUSTINE DIRECTORIES TO INCLUDE

Chapin's Handbook of St. Augustine, by Elias Nason, M. M., George H. Chapin, Publisher. St. Augustine, Florida, 1884.

St. Augustine Directory 1886. Abstracted from: Webb's Jacksonville and Consolidated Directory of Representative Cities of East and South Florida, 1886.

Elliott's Florida Encyclopedia or Pocket Directory. Jacksonville, Florida: Times-Union Book and Job Office, 1889.

Florida State Gazetteer and Business Directory. New York: South Publishing Company, 1886-7.

History Guide and Directory of St. Augustine. St. Augustine: The Record Company, 1904.

AUTHOR'S INTERVIEWS:

Carol Bradshaw (August 2001)
Shirley Browning (August 2001)
Bruce Chappell (August 23, 2001)
Peggy Caraway Cottle (April 2000 and July 2001)
George W. Gibbs, IV (2001)
Mary Gibbs Smethurst Grant (June 11, 2001)
Virginia Hassenflu (1999)
Betsy Haynes (July 2001)
Latrell E. Mickler (August 2001)
Eleanor Mitchell (October 2001)
Michele Perry (March 2000)
Ramelle Petroglou (July 25, 2001)

Dr. William L. Proctor (January 27, 2002)
Yvonne Punnett (2000)
Peggy Ready (March 2000)
Patty Steder (2000)
Katherine A. "Kat" Twine (1988, 2002)
Henrietta Whiteman, *Also known as*
    Henrietta Mann (1991)

INDEX

Cendoya, Governor Manuel, 20, 22
Chapman, Harkness and Company, 86
Charles V, King, 13
Charleston, South Carolina, 69, 92
Charlotte Harbor, 13
Chavas, Brook, 115
Chavas, George W., 115
Cherokee Garden Club, 137
Chesterfield, 46
Chiricahua Apaches, 113
Choate's Sanitarium, 97
City Gate, 77, 131, 132, *133*, 141
City of God, The, 130
Civil Rights demonstrations, 8
Civil War, 26, 47
Clark and Sanford, 89
Clark, Pearl, 115
Clark, Petronilla "Pet," 115
Clark, Theodore "Red," 115
Clark, Vondalyn "Von," 115
Cleveland, Ohio, 89, 90, 91
Clinch Street, 75
Coles, David J., 27
Colonial Dames Board of Managers, 133
Colonial Dames of America, 137
Colonial Dames, 132
Colt, Leonora Fatio, 72
Concepción, Doña Maria, 57, 58, 60
Consejo de Indias, 22
Cook, Margaret, 69, 70, 73
Cook, Mrs., 36
Cook, Samuel, 69
Cooper, Reverend James Henry, 115
Cooper's Hall, 115
Cordova and Valencia Streets, 106
Cordova Hotel, 136
Cordova Street, 120
Corsica, 23, 66
Cottle, Peggy Caraway, 8, *139*, 142
Cowford, 44
Cross and Sword, 18
Cuba, 48, 52
Cucarella, Ramon, 63, 64
Cumberland Island, Georgia, 58
Custer, George Armstrong, 117

D
Daughters of the American Revolution (DAR), The, 131, 134, 137
Dawson, Yukon Territory, 78, 79
Day, Louella, MD. *See* McConnell, Luella Day
Day, Luella. *See* McConnell, Luella Day
Day, Lyonell M. *See* McConnell, Luella Day
Day, Lyonella Murat. *See* McConnell, Luella Day
Daytona, Florida, 100
de Hita, Royal Engineer Manuel, 131, 134
Deagan, Dr. Kathleen, 84
Delaney, Lieutenant Guillermo, 62, 64
Delores Mestre, Maria de los. *See* Andreu, Maria
Diamond Lil. *See* McConnell, Luella Day
Dickens, Charles, 52
Diggs, Reverend Franklin P., 115
Dimick, Clarissa. *See* Gibbs, Clarissa Anderson
Dimick, John Cochran, 129
Dimick, John, 129
Dismukes, Elizabeth (Mrs. John), 132
Doctor's Lake, 42
Dummett, Anna, 123
Dunham, David L., 73
Dunham, Judge David R., 137
Dunlawton, 71

E
East Florida Gazette, 50, 52
El Escribano, 22, 27
Esther (schooner), 42
Evans, Maria. *See* Evans, Mary
Evans, Mary, 38, 39
Everglades, 51
Evergreen Cemetery, 56
Examiner, The, 30

F
Fairbanks, Clarissa C. *See* Anderson, Clarissa Cochran Fairbanks
Fatio Jr., Francis Philip, 72
Fatio, Eliza, 72
Fatio, Louisa, 72, 74
Fatio, Sophia, 72

Felix, William, 26
Fellowship Hall, 108
Fenwick, David, 38
Fernandina, Florida, 43, 51, 125
Flagler College, 142
Flagler Hospital Auxiliary, 137
Flagler Hospital, 128
Flagler Museum, Henry Morrison, 107, 108
Flagler Nursery School, 107, 108
Flagler, Anne Caroline "Carrie," 85, 86, 87, 94
Flagler, Carrie, 87, 88, 91
Flagler, Elizabeth Caldwell Morrison, 85, 86, 87, 88
Flagler, Henry "Harry" Harkness, 90, 102
Flagler, Henry Morrison, 8, 73, 74, 85, 88, 90, 91, 94, 99, 105, 124, 126
Flagler, Ida Alice Shourds, 94, 95, 96, 97, 98, 126, 127
Flagler, Isaac, 85, 86
Flagler, Jennie Louise. *See* Benedict, Jennie Louise Flagler Hinckley
Flagler, Mary Harkness, 86, 87, 88, 89, 91, 92, 94, 102
Flagler, Mary Lily Kenan. *See* Bingham, Mary Lily Kenan Flagler
Florida East Coast Railroad, 100
Florida House, 136
Florida Keys, 16
Florida National Guard, 141
Florida Press Association's Hall of Fame, 137
Florida State Historical Society, 137
Florida Women's Press Club, 137
Florida's Flagler, 95
Forrester, Gerardo, 40
Fort Ann, New York, 53
Fort Caroline, 15
Fort George Island, 44, 45, 47, 48, 125
Fort George plantation, 48
Fort Gordon, Georgia, 140
Fort Green, 75
Fort Marion, 33, 51, 74, 124
Fort Pierce, 100
Fountain of Youth, 8, 77, 81, 82, 83, 84

ABOUT THE AUTHOR

K aren Harvey has been fascinated by St. Augustine's history since moving to the Oldest City in 1978. Her first book, *St. Augustine and St. Johns County: A Pictorial History*, is popular with locals deeply rooted in the heritage of the town as well as visitors eager for more knowledge. *America's First City: St. Augustine's Historic Neighborhoods*, guides even those who live in the Ancient City around historically and architecturally significant sites and houses. *Oldest Ghosts: St. Augustine Haunts* adds a supernatural touch to history. Other works include anniversary celebration books for the century-old Flagler Hospital and Memorial Presbyterian Church. Museum scripting includes copy for exhibits about the Minorcan migration and the U.S. Coast Guard in St. Augustine during World War II.

Harvey's play *Conquest and Colonization* educates and entertains audiences about the founding of the First City.

Research of the various time periods from 1565 to the present introduced Harvey to the women depicted in *Daring Daughters*.